Common Sense Spirituality

THE ESSENTIAL WISDOM OF DAVID STEINDL-RAST

DAVID STEINDL-RAST

EDITED AND WITH INTRODUCTIONS BY
ANGELA IADAVAIA

FOREWORD BY JOAN CHITTISTER, OSB

A Crossroad Book
The Crossroad Publishing Company
New York

The Crossroad Publishing Company
16 Penn Plaza – 481 Eighth Avenue, Suite 1550
New York, NY 10001

Printed in the United States of America.

The text of this book is set in 11/14.5 Sabon.
The display faces are Engravers' Gothic, Voluta Script, and Gill Sans.

Cataloging-in-Publication Data is available from
the Library of Congress
ISBN-13: 978-0-8245-2479-1

1   2   3   4   5   6   7   8   9   10   12   11   10   09   08

Contents

IN SEARCH OF QUESTIONS
TOO BIG FOR ANSWERS

Someone wrote on a wall once, "If you expect to find an answer to your question, you have simply not asked a big enough question." In *Common Sense Spirituality*, Brother David Steindl-Rast teaches us to ask the right questions, the big questions in life.

The great enquiries of life are not children's riddles. Good thinkers do not expect to resolve them. They are simply the subjects serious thinkers spend their lives exploring so that all the other lesser questions of life can have a launching pad from which to commence their pursuit. Questions like What shall I do? Where shall I go? What are my priorities? are all issues that depend in the first place on what I think life is about and goodness is made of and meaning requires if we are to be truly alive, truly spiritual.

In *Common Sense Spirituality*, Brother David leads us through these slippery dimensions of life with gentle persistence, with spiritual depth. And with common sense. Never have we needed such guidance more.

We live in a very strange world now. It is a world of dazzling technological and scientific achievement. It is, as a result, a world of increasing complexity and confusion.

The more we discover about the mechanics of life, it seems, the less we are certain of the meaning of life, the purpose of life, the essence of life. It is a world, in fact, made strange by our own making.

A people enamored of science and skeptical of religion, we are, nevertheless, unsatisfied by science and tempted to substitute magical thinking for the mysteries of religion. We make for ourselves a vending-machine God and live torn between the verities of science and the spiritual values of religion. And that is strange, indeed, since neither is intended to be the answer to the other, however much we try to make them so.

As a result, we do not know where the world of science begins or where the world of religion ends. We want science to confirm things of the spirit for us, and we want religion to explain the origin of the world to us. Neither of them is up to the task.

Worst of all, we confuse one with the other. We want science, which deals with matter, to explain God to us. We want religion, which deals with the spirit, to be an authority on the biological nature of life.

In the end, we make a thing of God and a god of science. We make "heaven" a place and earth the center of the universe. And that's when the confusion and the complexity set in; that's when we begin to lose faith in both. What shall we believe about either heaven or earth when what we have thought of both of them is equally impossible and impertinent. God is bigger than an adult Disneyland designed to reward rulekeepers, and the earth is a speck in the universe too small to explain something as great as the end and purpose of creation.

No wonder we have come to the point where we consider science dangerous and religion spurious. We have asked the wrong things of both and in the doing of it, have misused both of them. Science is simply no substitute for religion and its pursuit of the transcendent. Religion, as much in awe of science as it may be, is not intended to be a self-help manual in biology.

It is precisely here at the crossroads between the two that this book takes up the challenge of marking the boundaries of both science and religion. And, in the doing of it, points up the real contribution each makes to the other.

This book does not pretend to give impossible answers or catechetical creeds. Instead, it enables us to rethink all the encrusted ideas humanity has conjured up to reduce God to our own dimensions. It stretches our vision of life and so it expands our insight into the necessary nature of God.

This book is a cry of the soul into the darkness of life that gives substance to faith and reason for hope. We cannot be who we are unless the God who made us is greater than we are with all our smallnesses of judgment and nationalism and sexism and absolutism.

The fact is that faith is not about facts. Faith is about surrendering to the goodness of the God who made a universe so purposeful in its existence, so unbounded in its magnificence, that it demands that we consider the munificence of a Creator who exceeds both ourselves and our universe.

Then, we find ourselves asea in God.

Then, we need to rethink both ourselves and our life.

Then, we discover ourselves in the grip of a God greater than the gods we have made of ourselves.

Then, we need a guide to the heart of a God too great to be thought, too present to be ignored.

Then, because we finally settle down to take the questions seriously, this book takes us seriously enough to lead us from the obvious to the metaphysical. Then, this book takes us to the height of our humanity in the most simple of human ways.

That's Brother David's gift and strength. He refuses to be obscure. He resists being dogmatic. He disdains being simplistic. He is unwilling to be obscurantist. He himself is the epitome of "common sense spirituality."

He simply takes us by the hand and invites us to rethink what the great thinkers of all time have posited in their own attempts to be their own most human selves. He invites us to live into an answer of our own rather than either swallow the answers of others or begin to live on the surface of life with neither awe of the questions nor respect for the breadth of the responses.

In the end, then, faith is not the refusal to face what cannot be answered. It is the commitment to think beyond what is to why it is. It is the conviction that we must stretch ourselves beyond what can only be seen to what it is meant to enable us to understand about what cannot be seen. About life. About goodness. About purpose. About creation. About the self. About God. About what constitutes "common sense spirituality."

This, then, is a book of big questions — about the mystical, the mystery, the cosmos, the spiritual, and the nature of obedience to it all. It is not only about the kind of questions that concern us all our lives but the kind of questions because of which we finally make a conscious commitment to live life one way rather than another.

The poet Rainer Maria Rilke puts it this way in his *Letters to a Young Poet* (1903):

> I would like to beg you, dear Sir, as well as I can, to have patience with everything unresolved in your heart and to try to love the questions themselves as if they were locked rooms or books written in a very foreign language.

This book of Brother David's will not resolve those questions. No, it does much more than that: it gives a reader the substance it takes to live these questions till, as Rilke says, "perhaps then, someday far in the future, you will gradually, without even noticing it, live your way into the answer." Then, perhaps, as Brother David has taught us, we will begin to contribute to the meaning of life for others by raising questions of our own.

Joan Chittister, OSB

A WORD ABOUT BROTHER DAVID

David F. K. Steindl-Rast was born on July 12, 1926, in Vienna, Austria. He spent his childhood in a small, predominately Catholic village nestled in the Alps, where he lived with his mother and two younger brothers. Celebrating religious feasts, attending a two-classroom school, and skiing on weekends defined the calendar for children of this village. It was here that he first experienced "the sacred, the cultural, and nature as one piece."

By 1938 when the Nazis invaded Austria, Brother David was attending a secondary boarding school in Vienna. Religion continued to be a dominant presence in his life, only now it was practiced underground. At a time when teenagers typically reject their religion, the opposite was true for him and his classmates. Pursuing their religion was their act of rebellion. Every year the graduating class in their school had to join the army, and almost every week those left behind attended a Mass for a former student who had been killed in the war. David was also drafted when he graduated, but he never was sent to the front. After a year, he escaped and was hidden by his mother.

After the war, David was given a copy of the Rule of St. Benedict, in which the tenet "keep death always before your eyes" caught his particular attention as did the authentic life proposed by this Father of Western monasticism. While this was one of the happiest times in David's life, he also knew then that unless death continued to be at the forefront of his awareness, he "would not be much alive anymore." This was on his mind as he became involved in art restoration and studied at the Vienna Academy of Fine Arts, where he received his master's degree. Drawn to the paintings of both children and primitive cultures, he then received a doctorate in psychology with a minor in anthropology from the University of Vienna.

In 1952 after joining his family who had emigrated to the United States, Brother David heard of a newly founded Benedictine community in Elmira, New York. It took only one visit for him to decide to join Mount Savior Monastery, of which he is now a senior member. Over the next decade, Brother David became a postdoctoral Fellow at Cornell University, where he also was the first Roman Catholic to hold the Thorpe Lectureship, following Bishop J. D. R. Robinson and Paul Tillich. Like the dozen monks at Mount Savior, he also enjoyed a rich spiritual and intellectual life in the monastery. Dorothy Day and members of the Catholic Worker as well as Daniel Berrigan, well known for his pacifist stance during the Vietnam War, were frequent visitors.

After twelve years of monastic training and studies in philosophy and theology in this milieu, Brother David was sent by his abbot to participate in Buddhist-Christian dialogue, for which he received Vatican approval in 1967. His Zen teachers were Hakkuun Yasutani Roshi, Soen Nakagawa Roshi, Shunryu Suzuki Roshi, and Eido

Shimano Roshi. He co-founded the Center for Spiritual Studies in 1968 and received the 1975 Martin Buber Award for his achievements in building bridges between religious traditions. Together with Thomas Merton, Brother David helped launch a renewal of religious life. From 1970 on, he became a leading figure in the House of Prayer movement, which affected some two hundred thousand members of religious orders in the United States and Canada.

For decades, Brother David divided his time between periods of a hermit's life and extensive lecture tours on five continents. His wide spectrum of audiences has included starving students in Zaire and faculty at Harvard and Columbia Universities, Buddhist monks and Sufi retreatants, Papago Indians and German intellectuals, New Age communes and naval cadets at Annapolis, missionaries on Polynesian islands and gatherings at the United Nations, Green Berets and participants at international peace conferences. Brother David has brought spiritual depth into the lives of countless people, whom he touches through his lectures, his workshops, and his writings.

He has contributed to a wide range of books and periodicals from the *Encyclopedia Americana* and the *New Catholic Encyclopedia,* to the *New Age Journal* and *Parabola* magazine. His books have been translated into many languages. *Gratefulness, the Heart of Prayer* and *A Listening Heart* have been reprinted and anthologized for more than two decades. Brother David co-authored *Belonging to the Universe* (winner of the 1992 American Book Award), a dialogue on new paradigm thinking in science and theology, with physicist Fritjof Capra. His dialogue with Buddhists produced *The Ground We Share:*

Everyday Practice, Buddhist and Christian, co-authored with Robert Aitken Roshi. His most recent books are *The Music of Silence,* co-written with Sharon LeBell, and *Words of Common Sense for Mind, Body, and Soul.*

Brother David contributed chapters or interviews to well over thirty books. An article by Brother David was included in *The Best Spiritual Writing, 1998.* His many audiotapes and videotapes are widely distributed.

At present, Brother David serves as founder/advisor to the worldwide "network for grateful living," through *www.gratefulness.org,* an interactive website with more than ten thousand visitors daily from more than 240 countries.

Editor's Note

These essays span more than thirty years of Brother David's evolving thought about what he has come to call Common Sense Spirituality. They illuminate our understanding of three essential themes:

- our peak or mystical experiences — an essential part of our spirituality that helps us find our own "firm basis of knowing,"

- the sacred traditions that are expressions of our spirituality — flawed but nevertheless with the potential to be lifelines to faith, hope, and love; and

- our response to our spiritual experiences — our willingness to let them define who we are and to shape our lives, meaningfully and with gratefulness.

The essays come from a variety of sources: published articles, interviews, and transcripts of talks. Many have been edited to eliminate repetitions. On occasion, points have been clarified or more relevant examples substituted. See *www.gratefulnesness.org,* where the original essays area available.

Special thanks to Patricia Carlson, executive director of A Network for Grateful Living, for her help in preparing this book. Special thanks also to Ariana Cox for her thoughtful insights and assistance, and to Paul Cox; he and Ariana, my children, are my best teachers. To Brother David — who has lived every word of these essays — my gratitude for his willingness to always come out of the hermitage and share his insights with us. Believing that we all belong on this planet together, he embodies Common Sense Spirituality.

PART ONE

Experiencing Our Spirituality

Brother David brings the ordinary to the extraordinary. Growing up in Austria during World War II and, in the subsequent decades, witnessing the loss of entire species of plants and animals, prompted him to realize that we are at a new threshold of moral consciousness — one that recognizes we all belong together and we must treat one another and our planet accordingly. We have reached a crucial point in history, he says, where there can be no exceptions. It would be immoral to believe otherwise.

But what does this mean for each of us personally? How can we renew our spirit so that we respond authentically and wholeheartedly to this need for belonging?

In this first group of essays, "Experiencing Our Spirituality," Brother David speaks to us from this new ground on which he firmly stands. From this vantage point, he takes us back to our starting points, where we can find our own firm basis for knowing and acting. To do so, he encourages us to rely on our spiritual senses for cues and guidance: to let go of our preconceived notions, to be open to discovery, and to see and listen with our hearts. Our own experiences — from seemingly everyday occurrences to our most treasured memories — will be the territory for exploration. Surprisingly, what can appear at times to be detours turn out to be the most direct ways to discover what we are looking for.

Slow reading and rereading of these essays are recommended. So is taking time to reflect on the poetry interspersed throughout the text and on our own personal experiences as Brother David often suggests. The attention and openness we bring will be richly rewarded.

CHAPTER I

SPIRITUALITY AS COMMON SENSE

This chapter lays the groundwork for the first group of essays, with its vision of what it means to be fully alive in mind, body, and spirit. This is, in essence, our spirituality and in order to make it part of who we are, Brother David appeals to our common sense. But his is not the typical notion of common sense in which a few practically minded people know how things work in this world. To him, common sense is a way of being attuned to the world around us. It is rooted in a knowing deep in our bones. It is everyone's birthright as well as responsibility to cultivate and practice. It is what we share in common with the whole of creation. This knowing that comes from our own experiences is at the core of Brother David's vision — and it must become part of our core.

By linking our spirituality and common sense, this essay gives us an opportunity to regain our footing. If we can connect our spirituality to common sense, and vice versa, we will have a true sense of direction for our journey.

As far back as we can trace, when speaking about spiritual matters, people used a term that simply means "life breath." Spirit means "breath" in Latin, Greek, and

Hebrew. Spirit is the very aliveness of life as we know it. It is as essential to life as the air we breathe. But what does this mean? We know this aliveness is more than just physical and mental capabilities. Think about the comment we often hear about a person's vitality, "He seems so alive!" Something more is at play here than just a steadier pulse or higher IQ.

The great spiritual traditions often use "aliveness" interchangeably with "mindfulness." This term emphasizes not so much mind as it stresses *fullness*. Aliveness is a fullness not only of the mind but also of body and spirit. This is quite a different notion from popular interpretations of mindfulness that create — or perpetuate — a common split between body and spirit. True spirituality, true aliveness, on the contrary, is deeply rooted in our bodies, something often underplayed or negated entirely in religions but readily identified in people regarded as deeply spiritual. Think of the Dalai Lama: his gestures and his belly laugh. The term "mindfulness" seems too limited in describing him, but what word would we use? When a word is lacking in a language, an insight is often lacking — in this case, the insight that full aliveness is mindfulness and body-fullness and that this full aliveness is at the heart of our spirituality.

Poetry provides us with examples of this extraordinary aliveness that we can relate to in our everyday life. A poem by William Butler Yeats celebrates one such moment. It sets an essentially religious experience in a context where we would not expect it. We are often disappointed in churches, mosques, and temples where we think we "should" have such an experience. But moments of aliveness don't come on command. When they come, we are, as C. S. Lewis puts it, "surprised by joy." So is Yeats in the poem "Vacillation, IV."[1]

It starts at an unlikely age for great aliveness — "My fiftieth year had come and gone" — and in most unpromising surroundings, he says:

> I sat, a solitary man,
> In a crowded London shop,
> An open book and empty cup
> On the marble table-top.

We all know that feeling of being solitary in the midst of a crowd, all the more lonely because of the crowd. The book is open. He seems to have lost interest in the middle of it. The cup is empty, and so seemingly are his thoughts. The cold stone table-top expresses perfectly his lack of any feelings at the moment. This man doesn't see what's going on around him. He gazes absentmindedly.

But something occurs unexpectedly and takes hold of him, a wondrous contrast to the emptiness with which the poem opens:

> While on the shop and street I gazed
> My body of a sudden blazed....

Notice that Yeats says he experiences this sudden awakening, his aliveness, in his body. He doesn't say anything about his mind or his thoughts. At that moment, he is not thinking. This awareness that makes the body blaze with aliveness vastly transcends thinking.

> ... And twenty minutes more or less
> It seemed, so great my happiness,
> That I was blessed and could bless.

The twenty minutes, "more or less," indicate that this was a timeless moment. But a tongue-in-cheek quality to the "more or less" also comes through. The experience is too overwhelming, and the poet has to distance himself by this colloquial expression. While he speaks merely of his "happiness," religious reality breaks in with the word "blessed." As in true spiritual experiences, the proof is in the fact that he can pass his blessed aliveness on to others. This is what religion (*re-ligio*, in Latin) is: literally the re-tying of ligaments that have been torn, bonds that connect us with all other creatures, with our own true self, and with the Divine. We are no longer lonely and solitary; we belong.

True aliveness is the expression of a profound belonging. Our body may not "blaze," but in some blissful moments, we do know, for one split second at least, that we belong. We know it in our bones. It's the ultimate way of knowing, not limited to thoughts, not limited to feelings, not limited to any other way of knowing. This is not the knowing we refer to in everyday conversations. It's not what Hui Tzu, the Confucian sage and stickler for words, meant by knowing. And this leads to an amusing exchange of words between him and the great Taoist master Chuang Tzu, an episode in which Thomas Merton delighted and which he translated in his book *The Way of Chuang Tzu* under the title "The Joy of Fishes":[2]

> Chuang Tzu and Hui Tzu
> Were crossing Hao river
> By the dam.
>
> Chuang said:
> "See how free

The fishes leap and dart:
That is their happiness."

Hui replied:
"Since you are not a fish
How do you know
What makes fishes happy?"

Chuang said:
"Since you are not I
How can you possibly know
That I do not know
What makes fishes happy?"

Hui argued:
"If I, not being you,
Cannot know what *you* know
It follows that you
Not being a fish
Cannot know what they know."

Chuang said:
"Wait a minute!
Let us get back
To the original question.
What you asked me was
'*How* do you know
What makes fishes happy?'
From the terms of your question
You evidently know I know
What makes fishes happy."

And then comes the decisive statement, a pronounce-
ment of greatest significance:

I know the joy of fishes
In the river
Through my own joy, as I go walking
Along the same river.

Is there any other way of knowing this? Obviously not. But consider what this implies.

Our most exhilarating knowing comes not from thinking but from the awareness of a shared aliveness — in this case, between Hui Tzu and the fish.

The Taoists called this shared aliveness "the Tao." This word simply meant "Way" or "Path," but Taoists stretched its meaning. We need a phrase for this reality, and "Common Sense" is the best one English has to offer. By calling this kind of knowing Common Sense, we are stretching the definition of what we normally mean by this phrase, but if we listen to it with fresh ears, it is an exceptionally good phrase. Often common sense is used to denote conventional assumptions, the exact opposite of full aliveness. But the Common Sense of which we now speak is so vibrant, so alive, so expansive that it gives a new color, a new flavor to everything we do, everything we are. It is a sensuous knowing, and it springs from what we have in common with the whole of creation. Inherent in our experiences is the realization that we are not separate bodies, but that in this universe, everything is interconnected, all is part of all. Out of this awareness springs the only knowing that makes sense. This knowing goes so deep that it is embodied in our senses and has no limits. The whole universe holds it in common. We need only plug into it.

Isn't this what Chuang Tzu is saying? By our own bliss we know the bliss of the fishes and the bliss of everything there is in the world. In that blissful moment we have reached a spiritual — fully alive — knowledge at the core of the world.

As we practice Common Sense, it becomes a basis for knowing, a basis for action. In Common Sense, action and thinking are closely connected. So Common Sense is more than thinking. It is a vibrating aliveness to the world, in the world, for the world. It is a knowing through belonging. And it becomes a basis for doing, for acting. To act in the spirit is to act as people act when they belong together. We all belong together in this "earth household," as Gary Snyder calls it so beautifully, and to live a spiritual life means to act as one acts in one's own house where one belongs together. This, and this alone, is moral action. All morality that was ever developed in any tradition in the world can be reduced to the principle of acting as one acts toward those with whom one belongs together.

It is often said that notions of what is moral and what is not differ completely from society to society. What is considered moral, even virtuous, in one is branded as immoral in another. But these are only surface contradictions. In its depth any moral law that was ever expressed basically says: "This is how one acts toward those with whom one belongs together." The differences are determined by where we draw the limit that separates those to whom we belong from those we consider outsiders.

Common Sense — precisely because it springs from the realization that we have our deepest identity in common — draws no limits. When you practice Common Sense, you practice a morality that includes everybody.

You behave toward everybody as one behaves when one belongs. When I was young, there was still room in our world for different sets of morality. Within my lifetime, we have passed a threshold: from now on, to draw a line and to exclude anybody is simply immoral. Even plants and animals must be included. We have been awakened to this consciousness that springs from Common Sense by the suffering of two World Wars and subsequent wars as well as from the loss of entire species of plants and animals that form essential parts of our earth's interdependent ecology. We have seen our globe from space, and the vision of it as an undivided blue-and-green whole reminds us that we are one earth family. This universally inclusive community is what Jesus meant by "the kingdom of God." By making community all-inclusive, he triggered an earthquake that is still reverberating in our world. The epicenter of this earthquake is the notion of authority.

Common sense rightly understood is authoritative. In fact it is the ultimate authority. Authority, which is so central to spirituality, is definitely one of those terms we need to clarify. One of our problems today is that this concept is so often misunderstood. Even when you go to the dictionary to look up "authority," the first meaning you will normally find is "power to command." This, however, is not at all its original meaning. The original meaning of authority is "a firm basis for knowing and acting." We still use the term frequently in that way. If we want to do some research, we go to an authoritative book. If we have health problems we go to a doctor who is known as an authority. We look for a firm basis for knowing and acting.

And where did Jesus place this firm basis? In God's commandments engraved in stone? In the religious leaders of his time? In himself and his own teachings? It may come as a surprise, but none of the above. Jesus placed the ultimate authority in the hearts of his hearers, not as a private possession but as participation in Common Sense. This is why his distinctive way of teaching is through parables.

His typical parable opens with a question, "Who of you doesn't know this already?" The obvious answer is, "Everybody knows it. It's common sense." And so the joke is on us, the hearers: If you know it so well, why don't you do it? You know, for instance, with what love *you* treat your children. Should God's love be less ardent and unflappable? Do you love one child more than the other? Why should God? Doesn't your love flow to the one in trouble? So does God's. In the telling and retelling, the parables have been turned into allegories and moral tales, but originally they were jokes that hinged on having Common Sense and not using it.

By this way of teaching, Jesus Christ created an authority crisis. People said, "This man speaks with authority, not like our authorities." What did they mean? When do you say that someone speaks with authority? When teachers put themselves on pedestals? No. Rather, when they make you stand on your own feet. Such teachers make you listen to the authoritative voice within your heart and strengthen you so that you come to know and follow that voice of Common Sense. But that will lead to trouble with authoritarians — and it did get Jesus into trouble. Even today, think of the base communities in Latin America, serving the poor under conditions of political upheaval that have often resulted in persecution and even martyrdom.

29

Jesus taught that the only legitimate use of authority is to build up those who are under authority. "The greatest among you ought to be the servant of all" (Mark 10:43–44). Those who have genuine authority do not need to put everybody down in order to keep themselves up. But this is exactly how authoritarians in Jesus' time worked — and so do authoritarians in all times. Thus, both the religious and the political authorities had to clamp down on Jesus. Anybody who makes people stand on their own two feet is dangerous for authoritarians. So they put him out of the way.

Yet that kind of spirit, because it is the ultimate Spirit, could not be killed and still goes on today. It is alive in the hearts of those who live in the spirit of Common Sense.

CHAPTER 2

THE MONK IN US

Our restlessness, the fears we acknowledge as well as push away, the long to-do lists we can't let go of — Brother David helps us understand that all of these define who we are spiritually. These preoccupations stand in contrast to our "peak moments" when suddenly everything makes sense — when, as he says, we lose ourselves and, in the process, find ourselves.

Fully appreciating our going back and forth between these two poles, Brother David offers an alternative in this essay. He stops time in the midst of our peak moments so we can tap into "the monk in us." Like monks, we can learn how to become more receptive to the lightning-quick flashes of insight that our peak moments reveal. We can learn from our own intuitive responses at these crucial moments in our lives. Like monks, we can let their meaning seep into all that we do and are. These moments are our stepping stones. Rather than grasping onto truth, these moments teach us how to let truth "hold" us.

The monk in us is very closely related to the mystic in us — and we are all meant to be mystics. We do a great disservice to mystics by putting them on a pedestal and thinking of them as unique. The truth is that every human being is a special kind of mystic. I am using the term "mysticism" in the strictest sense, as the experience of deep union with Ultimate Reality — those moments of blissful wholeness and harmony that break through to us every once in a while. No one experiences Ultimate Reality in the same exact way, but we are all called to experience this communion and to become the mystics that only we can be.

What does distinguish mystics, however, is their willingness to give these experiences the central place they deserve in our lives. Mystics allow these moments to influence how and what they do and, in so doing, to give meaning to their lives. Monks are also drawn to the challenge of translating this bliss of universal communion into their daily living. Everything in their environment — the rhythm of their day, the giving of enough time to what deserves time, their attention to work as well as prayer — is geared toward developing the inner attitude that we commonly refer to as mindfulness or deliberate living. Their environment enables them to be receptive to experiencing this communion — this full aliveness — which, in turn, creates a meaningful life.

Children have an instinctive openness and longing to find meaning. We see it in their curiosity, in how they become totally engaged in whatever they are looking at or listening to or licking or playing with. They are not distracted or thinking about what they are going to do next. They live in the present moment. Some cultures value and encourage this openness. Many Native American tribes, for example, hold as their ideal of a well-educated child one who "ought to be able to sit and look when there is nothing to be seen ... and able to sit and listen when there is nothing to be heard."

Unfortunately, in our culture, this openness tends to get quickly lost or at least overshadowed at an early age, a result most likely of our adult preoccupation with our overly "purposefulness" lives. Think how often almost every waking minute of the day — for children and adults — is scheduled with prescribed activities — and all in allotted time slots. We have become in a sense a lopsided people, scurrying about, doing what we have to do, but in the process, shutting down our connection to that which gives shape to and meaning in our lives. If we want to experience full aliveness, become the mystics we are meant to be, we have to learn to open ourselves, to give ourselves to what we are doing. And this is, by nature, the attitude of the child, and by training, the attitude of the monk.

By no means do I want to play what I call *purpose* against *meaning* or *meaning* against *purpose*. This is not an either/or proposition. Purpose and meaning go together, but we need to distinguish how they are different. The best way to do this is to think about a situation in which you have to carry out a particular purpose and see what the inner dynamics are and then compare this to a situation in which something becomes meaningful to you. When you have to accomplish a particular purpose, the main thing is that you have to take things in hand. You have to handle the matter, to come to grips with the situation, to keep things under control — otherwise you are never quite sure that you are going to accomplish your purpose. You have a task to do, you apply yourself to it, and then it is done.

By contrast, if you are curious and open to meaning, you allow something to happen to you without trying to hold on. You find yourself using expressions in which you are perfectly passive or at least more passive than when accomplishing a purpose. "Responsive" is a more precise description. No longer are you the one who keeps things under control or handles the situation. Instead the experience does something to you. You might say, "This really did something to me." "It really touched me," or if it is very strong, "It hit me over the head!" or, "It swept me off my feet!" When something becomes meaningful, you respond by giving yourself to it. In that moment, it — whatever it may be — is revealing its meaning to you.

The psychologist Abraham Maslow studied these moments as part of his research on what he calls "peak experiences." He describes them as transient moments of self-actualization. I think of them simply as moments that "make life worth living." You can also think of the term "peak experience" literally. These moments are elevated above your normal experience. They are always experienced as a point in time, just as the peak of a mountain is always a point. They may be a high peak or a low peak; the decisive thing is that they come to a peak, a point of vision or insight. When you are up on top of a peak you have a better vision. You can look all around. While you are still going up, part of the vision or the horizon is hidden by the peak you are ascending. But once on the peak, you get an insight into meaning; there's a moment in which meaning really touches you. That is the kind of insight that I am referring to now. It's not finding a solution to a concrete package of problems. You are not setting any limits to your insight; it is simply a moment of limitless insight.

Try to remember very concretely an experience in which something deeply touched you, in which you were somehow elevated above a normal level. Generalities won't do. And it is not necessary to have had a gigantic peak experience — they are very rare in one's life. An anthill is also a peak, so anything that comes to a peak will do for our purposes. If these experiences are, as it appears to me they are, the core of the mystical experience, then even in little anthill-type peak experiences there will be found the essence of the monk in each of us.

In choosing an experience, you might be thinking, "Gee, nothing really happened." Well, that is a profound insight, because if you allow *nothing* to happen, that's the greatest mystical experience. But you may find yourself inclined to use expressions such as, "Oh, I just lost myself. I lost myself when I heard this passage of the music," or, "I just lost myself looking at that little sandpiper running after the waves; as soon as the waves come the sandpiper runs back and then the sandpiper runs after the waves." You lose yourself in such an experience, and after you lose yourself for a little while, you are never quite sure again whether the waves are chasing the sandpiper or whether the sandpiper is chasing the waves or whether anybody is chasing anybody. But something has happened there and you lost yourself in that moment.

And then, strangely, you find yourself saying that in this experience in which you lost yourself, you were for once truly yourself. "That was a moment when I was really myself, more so than at other times. I was just carried away." It's a poetic expression. Certain things in life cannot be expressed in any way except poetically, and so these expressions enter into our everyday language. But then you find again the paradox, because while you say, "I was carried away," you also realize that "I was more truly in the present than I am at any other time." Like most of us, most of the time, I am not really fully present where I am. Instead, I'm 49 percent ahead of myself, focused on what's going to come, and 49 percent behind myself, hanging on to what has already passed. There's hardly any of me left to be present. Then something seemingly insignificant comes along — a little sandpiper or the rain on the roof — that sweeps me off my feet, and, for one split second, I'm completely present where I am. I'm carried away and I'm present where I am. I lost myself and I found myself, truly myself.

Perhaps these paradoxes are not as strange as they seem. Paradoxes must be present in any mystical experience, which is, after all, a way of comprehending unity. Two apparently contradictory things come together in a way we could not ordinarily comprehend. Here is another paradox. Many people choose an experience in which they were alone — a moment alone in their room or walking on the beach or out in the woods or maybe on a mountaintop. In one of those experiences they find that even though they were alone — and, paradoxically, not so much in spite of being alone, but because of being so truly alone at that moment — they were united with everything and everybody. If there were no other people around with whom you could experience this connection, you may feel united with the trees, if there were any, or with the rocks or with the clouds or with the water or with the stars or with the wind or whatever it was. It may have felt as if your heart was expanding, as if your being was expanding to embrace everything, as if the barriers were in some way broken down or dissolved and you were one with all. In retrospect perhaps you realize that you didn't miss any of your friends at the peak of your peak experience. Yet a moment later, you might have said, "I wish that so-and-so could be here and experience this beautiful sunset or to hear this music." But at the peak of your peak experience, you typically weren't missing anybody because at that moment, you were united with all. There was no point in missing anybody. You reached that center of which religious tradition sometimes speaks of the convergence of everybody and everything.

But we can also turn this paradox — when I am most truly alone I'm one with all — around. Some of you may have been thinking of an experience in which part of the peak experience was that you felt one with all in an enormous group of people. Maybe it was a liturgical celebration, a peace march or demonstration, a concert, or a play — some gathering where part of the enjoyment was that you felt that everybody there was one heart and one soul and that everybody there was experiencing this same thing. This may not have been objectively true. You may have been the only person to experience this connection. But even in this situation we turn the paradox around. When you are one with all, you are really alone. You are singled out as if that particular word of the speaker or selection of music, or whatever it was, were addressed to you personally. You almost blush. "Why is he talking about me? Why is he singling me out?" or "This particular passage of this particular symphony was composed for me, and this lavish performance is all for me, right here." You are singled out; you are perfectly alone. And we come to see that there is no contradiction here either.

When you are really alone you are one with all — even the word "alone" in some way alludes to that — all one, one with all, truly alone.

I'd like to consider a third paradox, which in some respects is the most important one. See again if it corresponds with your own experience. When the peak experience hits you, in a flash of insight everything makes sense. This is very different from laboriously finding the answer to some problem. We think we'll get the answer to this problem, but the moment we have the answer to this problem, several others arise. So we think, okay, we'll follow this other problem to its end until what finally happens is that we realize this chain is a circle, taking us around and around, from the last answer to the first question.

In a peak experience, somehow intuitively you become aware of the fact that to find the answer you have to drop the question. For a split second you drop the question, and the moment you do, the answer is there. It seems that the answer was always trying to get through. The only reason it couldn't is because you were so busy asking questions. Why should this be? Why should this happen in a peak experience? There seems a vast disproportion between cause and effect in these moments. I was doing nothing but looking at a sandpiper running after the waves and running away from the waves; I was doing nothing but lying awake and listening to the rain drumming on the roof; why should suddenly everything make sense?

There's another way of trying to approach this. You see the sandpiper and something in you says a wholehearted yes, or you hear the rain and your whole being says yes to it. It's a special kind of yes. It's an unconditional yes that this moment draws out of you from deep down and the moment you have said an unconditional yes to any part of reality, you have implicitly said yes to everything. It is a yes to everything that you normally compartmentalize into good and bad and black and white and up and down. In this unconditional yes, all of a sudden, everything falls into a pattern, and you say yes to all of life, to the "pattern" that is life.

What are we to make of these moments then when reality caught us unaware and we were able to respond wholeheartedly, unconditionally? If you can relate to these moments just described, if something in you can say, "Yes, this applies to my own experience," than you have experienced during some very important moments in your life what it is that makes monastic life tick. Remember that mystics differ from us merely in their willingness to accept mystical moments with all they offer and demand. And that is what monastic life is about. It helps us to cultivate that mystical attitude, that openness toward meaning that we experience in our peak experiences and that gives meaning to all of life.

Let me take this parallel with monastic life one step further. Monastic life is really about harvesting the seeds of the three paradoxes that we just discussed. The responses that these moments spontaneously elicited from us are what monks commit to develop in their vows of poverty, celibacy, and obedience. People often think of these vows as a denial of the senses, but the asceticism of monastic life is similar to the training that a runner or artist undergoes. They do without some things because they have made a commitment to something important to them, which is part of them. In this case, the monk makes a commitment to his spirituality.

If anybody has experienced the paradox that when we lose ourselves we find ourselves, then that person has inner access to the very heart of what a *life of poverty* is meant to be for the monk. A life of poverty has only one goal, and that is simply to lose yourself and so find yourself. This is different from saying, "I lost myself in order to find myself." Expectations and purposefulness are implied in this statement, which are contradictory to the true spirit of poverty. I lose myself and I discover that I have found myself. The monk spends his life cultivating this seed. The harvest is nothing else but what the seed was, because you never harvest anything but what you sow; that is, you lose yourself and so find yourself — only more so.

If you take the second paradox — that when I'm truly alone I'm one with all and when I'm really one with all I'm alone — you have the seed of a *life of celibacy*. Again, what lies between the seed and the harvest is simply ascetic effort that can take many, many different forms. One could make a very good case that married life is another road toward the same goal of being one with all and truly alone. You are not just half of a pair nor is marriage an egotism for two. You are one with yourself, truly alone and one with all — not only with your partner, but one with all.

The third paradox lies at the root of what we call *obedience*. The first thing that we think of is that you do what somebody else tells you to do. That's a time-honored and very helpful ascetic means toward the end, but to get stuck in this would be fruitless. If it is just a matter of replacing my self-will with somebody else's self-will, I would rather have my own self-will; it is much closer to home. The whole idea is to get beyond self-will altogether, because self-will is the one thing that gets between us and listening. Obedience means literally a thorough listening; *ob audire* means to listen thoroughly or, as the Jewish tradition says, "to bare your ear." The ear locks have to be removed so that you can listen thoroughly. That's obedience in the Old Testament. In many, many forms, in many, many languages, the word for "obedience" is an intensive form of the word "listening" — *horchen, ge-horchen; audire, ob-audire;* etc.

In other words, obedience, doing what somebody else tells you, may be used as an ascetic means to get over self-will that is solely focused on having your own ideas and blueprints. It's a means to drop all this and to look at the whole and to praise the whole, as Augustine says. But the decisive thing is to learn to listen, and very often doing somebody else's will can be a hindrance to learning to listen; you just become a marionette pulled on strings. This is very important in the context of finding meaning, the context in which we see the mystical experience. When you find something meaningless you say that it is absurd. But when you say "absurd," you've given yourself away — because the term *absurdus* is the exact opposite to *ob-audiens*. *Absurdus* means absolutely deaf. So if you say something is absurd, you are simply saying, "I am absolutely deaf to what this is going to tell me. The totality is speaking to me, and I am absolutely deaf." There is nothing out there that's deaf; you cannot attribute deafness to the source of the sound. You are deaf. You can't hear. So the only alternative that all of us have in any form of life is to replace an absurd attitude with an obedient attitude. It takes a lifetime to get just a little way into this.

What this all comes down to is that there is a lot more to life than just the phenomena. There is a whole dimension of life to which we have to listen with what the Bible and many religious traditions call the "heart." The heart is the whole person, not just the seat of our emotions. The kind of heart that we are talking about here is the heart in the sense in which a lover says, "I will give you my heart." That doesn't mean I give you part of myself; it means I give myself to you. The heart involves the whole person: the intellect, the will, and emotions. So when we speak about wholeheartedness, a wholehearted approach to life, mindfulness, that is the attitude through which alone we give ourselves to meaning.

A technical term that is mostly used in the Catholic tradition and is a good term for this is "recollection" — to be recollected, to live recollectedly. It means the same thing as mindfulness, whole-heartedness, openness to meaning. Recollectedness is "concentration without elimination," to use a phrase from T. S. Eliot, a paradox, because concentration normally limits. But if you can accomplish concentration without elimination, if you can combine the attitude of focusing on something and yet be totally open without horizons, then you have accomplished what recollection means. Then you have accomplished what all of monastic life in any of its traditions is after — recollected living, mindful living, deliberate living. Thoreau, when he went to Walden Pond, would refer to going to "live deliberately." That means recollectedly in this sense.

The decisive thing by which you will recognize monastic life is that it is recollected life, wholehearted life. It is through wholehearted living that meaning flows into our lives. That means that while we are engaged in purpose we keep ourselves open enough to let meaning flow into our lives. We don't get stuck in purpose.

To understand monastic life — recollected or wholehearted life — from another perspective we can look at purpose and meaning again, this time in relation to work and play. Work in the narrowest sense is closely related to purpose. You work until you have accomplished your purpose. You sweep the floor until it is swept. You research and write until your report is complete. You exercise until you clock in three miles. Play does not aim at any particular purpose. Play has meaning in it self. You don't sing in order to get a song sung — you sing in order to sing. And you don't dance, as Alan Watts pointed out, to get somewhere; you dance in order to dance. It has all its meaning in itself. What we are aiming for is leisure, which bridges the gap between work and play. Leisure is doing your work — doing anything you do — with the attitude of play. That means bringing to the moment at hand what is most important about playing, namely, that you do it for its own sake and not just to get it done. The monastic attitude is to do anything we do with whole-hearted attention — with an openness to meaning.

We typically assume that leisure is a privilege for those who can take time for it, but it is not. Leisure is a virtue. It is the virtue of those who give time to whatever takes time and give as much time as it deserves. In so doing, we are working leisurely, finding meaning in work and becoming fully alive. If we have a strict work mentality we are only half alive. We are like people who only breathe in, and suffocate. It really doesn't make any difference whether you only breathe in or only breathe out; you will suffocate in either case. That is a very good pointer toward the fact that we are not playing off work against play or purpose against meaning. The two have to come together. We have to breathe in and breathe out and so we keep alive. This is really what we are all after and is what all religion must be about — aliveness.

One last question: Why are we not more alive? The answer is one word — fear. One thing is at the root of everything that distorts or destroys life — and that is fear. We are simply afraid to be alive. Why are we afraid to be alive? Because to be alive means giving ourselves, and when we really give ourselves, we never know what's going to happen to us.

As long as we keep everything nicely under control, everything purpose-directed, everything in hand, there's no danger, but no life either. A world in which we could keep everything under control would be so boring that we'd die of boredom. We experience that in little ways every day. We get scared and we keep things under control, but the moment we really get them under control we get bored. It's true of interpersonal relationships. We think we know someone so well that we can predict how he or she will act. That's all right to a certain point; it's very reassuring. But then comes the point where it is boring, and so we seek to add a little adventure. Now the moment we have adventure we have danger; we have risk. We can't have adventure without risk, and so we open ourselves a little bit. We relax our grip a little bit, and, the moment we do, everything gets very interesting and adventuresome but also scary. The next thing we know, we're clamming up again and we're trying to get things under control again. So we go back and forth, back and forth, between these two poles all our lives, and that's really what spiritual life is all about. That's what religion is all about — the fear of losing ourselves and what it is that overcomes that fear.

The thing that overcomes fear is courage. But courage is our contemporary expression for what traditional religion in all its different branches called faith. We have wrong notions about faith; we think that faith means believing something. Yes, it does mean believing something. If we really trust in a person, if we really have faith in a friend, that also implies that we are believing some things about that friend. But that is very secondary, and if we get stuck in that we'll never get at the root of faith. Having faith does not mean subscribing to some dogmas or to some articles of faith or anything like that. Faith ultimately is courageous trust in life. The particular form that our religious faith takes depends entirely on the time and the place and the social structure and the cultural forms into which we are born, and there is an infinite variety of these. But the essence of our faith is the same at all times and in places, and it is the courageous trust in life.

Faith versus fear — that is the key issue of religion. That is also the key of our attitude toward truth. We know that religion has something to do with truth, but it isn't the truth that we can grab and grasp and take home with us. If we grasp and rigidly hold certain truths, next we will clash with everybody who does not hold those truths. When it comes down to it, everybody holds a different truth; there are as many different truths as

45

there are people around. So if we insist on the truth being something that we must hold, then we are at odds with everybody else in the world. But the real truth that we are after is something that holds us; it holds us when we give ourselves, in those moments when we really open ourselves. There is only one truth, and it takes hold of each person in an individual way. There must be an infinite variety of ways in which truth takes hold of all of us because in that variety the unity of truth blossoms forth. And it is beautiful and we must assert it and we must celebrate it. That's what life is and that's what religious life is, but it's giving ourselves to the truth, not taking the truth, grasping the truth, holding the truth. It's only the truth to which we give ourselves that will make us free. The one truth for all of us is that we must have courage to give ourselves to truth. Fear hangs on. Fear always grabs for something. The moment we get fearful, we grasp for something with the reflex of the monkey that grabs for the mother. This fear is deeply in all of us, genetically; it is the fear that makes us hang on to something. Faith is precisely the letting go and letting truth hold us. Each of us can experience this fearlessness; we need only to recall our peak experiences when intuitively the "monk in us" responded.

CHAPTER 3

ART AND THE SACRED

The sense of awe that sometimes takes us by surprise provides the connecting link between art and the sacred for Brother David. In its "strange mix of fear and fascination," this awe can be so strong that we must transform it into a rite of worship, one that may bring us to our knees or to new depths of artistic expression. Both responses require an openness that takes us beyond our own narrow definition of order. Both elicit an inner acknowledgment and acceptance, a "worshipful Yes of blessing."

In this essay, Brother David focuses on several artists' courageous openness in the face of horrific heartbreak and loss. Events pushed these artists beyond their ordinary limits to deeper realms of understanding and even hope. The challenge is no different for us when we respond to our own heartbreaks and loss: to let the sacred take shape in us and re-create us.

Remember when we were children and got one of those big shiny red apples? We would say to our mother, "You take the first bite," because we couldn't get our teeth into it. Once a little bite was taken out of it, we could manage.

As I looked at the theme of the topic, Art and the Sacred, I realized that art alone would already be too big to get my teeth into. And the sacred would be too big. So I will concentrate, humbly, on the "and." I would like to use words of poets and one painting — Picasso's *Guérnica* — to illustrate points about the link between art and the sacred. My aim is to move to that place where the two are linked and to help each one of us take our position there.

A passage that Gilbert Kerr, editor of the *Harvard Advocate*, wrote about the poet W. H. Auden might be a helpful place to start. Auden believed, said Kerr, that "a poet feels the impulse to create a work of art when the passive awe provoked by an event is transformed into a desire to express that awe in a rite of worship." He doesn't even say into a "work of art." He says a "rite of worship." Art comes in through the back door, as it were, when, he adds, "to befit homage, this rite must be beautiful." So we start with an awe-inspiring event. Then what Kerr calls "the passive awe" of this experience is transformed by the artist. That rite of worship, in words, is poetry. In movement, it is dance. In color and line, it is painting. In all these forms there is a rite of worship.

For our understanding we could separate this awe-inspiring event, or moment, into three phases. The first is stillness. In order to face reality, in whatever form it may be, we have to hold still. What kind of stillness is meant here will become clearer, I hope, when we read a few passages from T. S. Eliot's *Four Quartets*. But at this moment it is important for us not to think about the examples or about artists, but to appeal to our own experience. What is necessary when we want to face reality is stillness. Each one of us knows the kind of stillness that is absolutely necessary to face reality. Stillness is a precondition for facing anything. When we are rushing around, automatically going about what we have to do, we do not have the steadiness or presence that is necessary to look at anything face to face.

The next phase of our moment of awe is discovery. Stillness is necessary for discovery, but there is also something else: the letting go of our preconceived notions. This is a deepening of the concept of stillness. It deserves to be mentioned specifically because no matter how still you are externally when you look at things, you are not really looking at them unless you disengage yourself from your preconceived notions and allow reality to impress you. The moment you open yourself to reality, the moment you allow it to do something to you, only then do you discover an order that is not your order. You discover in things an order that existed millions and millions of years before we ever came around; in persons, you discover that mysterious order of the Other.

The third phase of facing reality that I would like to single out is what we might call the Yes. It is not enough to be still; it is not enough to open yourself for discovery. To fully face reality you have to say Yes. This is the Yes of blessing. It is not necessarily the "yes" of approval. Approval may not be the appropriate response in a given situation, but blessing is always appropriate. And blessing in this sense is an inner Yes. It is, as I hope you will see, a worshipful Yes, the essence, in fact, of worship.

If we reread our initial text once more, this time in the light of these three steps to facing reality, the idea these words convey seeps in a little deeper. "The poet feels the impulse to create a work of art when the passive awe provoked by an event is transformed into a desire to express that awe in a rite of worship. To be fit homage, this rite must be beautiful."

To be sure we are speaking the same language, it may be helpful to examine the key words in the quotation. With "art," for instance, the important thing is to recognize that we are talking about making something, the act of creation. Whether it be poetry or painting or architecture or dance, it is a making. And yet art is distinguished from crafts, which are characterized by making things for a purpose. "Art" in the sense that we have been talking about is distinguished by an emphasis on meaning rather than purpose, on celebration rather than use. Art in this case is a celebration, ultimately, of the superfluous. The superfluous is somehow celebrated with the deep intuition that nothing is more important to us humans than the superfluous.

What matters with the *sacred* is awe, in the sense of a strange and inexplicable fusion of fear and fascination. You see it when a very small child stands at the ocean and the waves are coming in. You see the little child torn between wanting to rush into the ocean and fearfully drawing back. Every time the wave comes, the child gets a little frightened, and every time the wave withdraws, the child runs up and gets closer. And then runs back again.

Beauty is a subject of endless potential. I would merely like to insist that we think of beauty not selectively but as an aspect of everything there is in all reality. Whatever is, is good. Whatever is, is true. Whatever is, is beautiful. That is what truth means: reality as faced by the intellect.

And beauty, in turn, is reality faced by the senses. Beautiful is, as St. Thomas said, the splendor of truth, the clarity everything has, if we would only see. If we could do just this: be still, open ourselves, and say that inner Yes, and allow that splendor to break forth without limit. It is our own limitations that determine the measure in which we are able to accept what is. This facing of reality with the Yes of blessing is worship. You do not have to add anything special to it. This facing of reality brings us to our knees. Kneeling is the position we feel to be most appropriate at that moment. The awe-struck kneeling is by itself an act through which meaning flows into our lives.

Now up to this point everything seems simple enough, a PG rating. No one would have too much difficulty with all this. But here comes a challenge. And that's why I refer to Picasso's *Guérnica,* which is one of the great pieces of art of our time.

It was provoked on April 29, 1937, when for the first time in history a squad of bombers wiped out a village. The timing for this saturation bombing, as historians have shown, was deliberately set during the busiest hours of the morning when everybody was out of their houses and in the market. The bombers came, and a few minutes later this village, unarmed, strategically unimportant, was simply wiped out. A few days later Picasso, under the tremendous shock of this experience, started sketching for *Guérnica.*

For us, the question this event imposes is decisive. Here was certainly an awe-inspiring event, but a terrible one. Here is something to which you can hardly say Yes. Or can you? What was it the artist said to this event? What was the inner gesture that produced a painting like this?

Only when we focus on this most difficult point where the "and" that stands between art and the sacred becomes almost impossible to deal with will we be able to maintain the link between the two. I must admit I have no glib answer at all. I am struggling with it, and I invite you to struggle with me. Struggle with these questions: How can we bless in the midst of disaster? In the midst of apathy? In the midst of destruction? In the midst of decay? In the midst of stupidity? In the midst of the fearfulness that lies at the root of so many terrible things?

And yet nobody can look long at Picasso's painting and fail to realize that it is a Yes. It is a Yes that includes and surpasses all the horror of the event captured in its imagery. How could Picasso say this Yes? Certainly he did not prettify the event and say, "Well, it wasn't really that bad. There were some nice things about it." He simply faced reality. He did nothing else but what we discussed earlier, only he did so in an extreme situation. He held still, but in this context, it is a very special kind of holding still. It demands extreme courage. He discovered order, but he didn't discover a facile order. He had the daring of a discoverer, the truth that there was some order he had not yet discovered, some order beyond what he might ever discover. He had the courage to bless, the courage to say yes in the midst of all this. This Yes, remember, is not necessarily one of approval, but it is an affirmation of reality.

All this might become clearer after reading three passages from Eliot's *Four Quartets*.[1] Although I address only a small segment of this lengthy poem, it nonetheless offers us something significant: the holding still, the poet confronting reality:

I said to my soul, be still, and wait without hope
For hope would be hope for the wrong thing; wait
    without love
For love would be love of the wrong thing; there is yet
    faith
But the faith and the love and hope are all in the
    waiting.
Wait without thought, for you are not ready for
    thought:
So the darkness shall be the light, and the stillness the
    dancing.

and a few lines earlier:

I said to my soul, be still, and let the dark come upon you
Which shall be the darkness of God.

There is the sacred. We can feel it. This first phase is no longer just stillness in general, but it is an explicit command: "Be still." That means have the courage to be still. "I said to my soul, 'be still.'" Not just externally quiet, but quiet in the ultimate sense of waiting without hope.

Just a very short space after that, there is another passage, about discovery.

Shall I say it again? In order to arrive there,
To arrive where you are, to get from where you are not,
You must go by a way wherein there is no ecstasy.
In order to arrive at what you do not know
You must go by a way which is the way of ignorance.

To arrive at what you do not know, at that order which is not your own, is discovery. But... "In order to arrive at what you do not know, you must go by a way which is the way of ignorance." The decisive point is to have the courage to go by the way of ignorance, by "the way in which we are not." That is real courage. To get from where you are not, "...you must go by a way wherein there is no ecstasy." That seems important because, linguistically, "ecstasy" — which comes from roots meaning "out of place" — is the opposite of "instant." You have to be in the present moment. That is how Eliot, in this context, speaks about confronting reality. To be really in the present moment, to immerse yourself in it, to allow it to do something to you, to expose yourself to it and not protect yourself with preconceived notions.

A final passage from the *Four Quartets* is about the Yes of blessing. Eliot expresses this Yes powerfully when he speaks about worship in confrontation with reality:

> If you came this way,
> Taking any route, starting from anywhere,
> At any time or at any season,
> It would always be the same: you would have to put off
> Sense and notion. You are not here to verify,
> Instruct yourself, or inform curiosity
> Or carry report. You are here to kneel....

Another clue to what this kneeling means stands at the end of a poem by W. H. Auden called "Precious Five."[2] It deals, stanza by stanza, with each of our five senses. After treating the five, Auden says in a final stanza:

> happy, precious five,
> So long as I'm alive
> Nor try to ask me what
> You should be happy for;

Think, if it helps, of love
Or alcohol or gold,
But do as you are told.
I could (which you cannot)
Find reasons fast enough
To face the sky and roar
In anger and despair
At what is going on,
Demanding that it name
Whoever is to blame:
The sky would only wait
Till all my breath was gone
And then reiterate
As if I wasn't there
That singular command
I do not understand,
Bless what there is for being,
Which has to be obeyed, for
What else am I made for,
Agreeing or disagreeing.

Bless what there is for being with the Yes of blessing. Be happy, precious five. Be happy. But happy in what sense? Again Eliot has a passage about that happiness:[3]

The moment of happiness — not the sense of well-
    being,
Fruition, fulfillment, security or affection,
Or even a very good dinner, but the sudden
    illumination —

All we need to do is hold still, be still, be open, listen. Then even the most shattering event may become transparent in a sudden illumination. The fourth section of "Little Gidding" in the *Four Quartets* describes a shattering event quite comparable to Guérnica. It deals with the bombing of London and was written during World War II. In these two stanzas Eliot makes the dive bombers transparent to the dove, symbol of the Holy Spirit who sends fire from the sky at Pentecost.[4]

> The dove descending breaks the air
> With flame of incandescent terror
> Of which the tongues declare
> The one discharge from sin and error.
> The only hope, or else despair
> Lies in the choice of pyre or pyre —
> To be redeemed from fire by fire.
> Who then devised the torment? Love.
> Love is the unfamiliar Name
> Behind the hands that wove
> The intolerable shirt of flame
> Which human power cannot remove.
> We only live, only suspire
> Consumed by either fire or fire.

This does something to our concept of God, I hope. It reminds me of what a Hassidic master said: "God is not an uncle. God is an earthquake!" And that earthquake is not something that happened out there in 1937 in Spain or in 1944 in London. It happened the last time we had some soul-shattering experience. It may happen whenever and wherever we hold still. And it will not only destroy but build up, if we can rise to a Yes of blessing.

Blessing is a creative encounter, for it is that basic gesture which, in biblical tradition, we predicate both of God and of ourselves. God blesses us. We bless God.

A time of crisis is a time to kneel, to open ourselves for blessing, and to bless. Thus, the sacred will take shape. In every crisis may we (as Rilke put it), "like the tongue between the teeth, remain, nevertheless, an organ of praise."[5]

CHAPTER 4

SACRAMENTAL LIFE:
TAKE OFF YOUR SHOES!

"To see all things aflame with divine fire," Brother David tells us, is the secret of sacramentality. If we can move beyond the visible and invisible barriers that we create for ourselves and instead see with the "eyes of our heart," then we too can be like Moses and encounter our own personal Burning Bush.

There is only one condition: we must take off our shoes. This is a gesture of thanksgiving that acknowledges that the ground on which we stand is holy. And, in the full cycle of "Experiencing Our Spirituality," going barefoot also brings a special grace. We not only are touched by God's healing power that comes to us through the earth; we are in touch with "God's unimaginable otherness in all things familiar."

Some insights of the heart are so deep that only a story can help to bring them home to ourselves or to share them with others. What we call in abstract terms "sacramental life" is one such example. While the story I have chosen comes out of the biblical tradition, its basic insight belongs to the common treasure of all religions and will be found in stories from many different traditions in the East as well as in the West.

Moses was looking after the flock of Jethro, his father-in-law, priest of Midian. He led his flock to the far side of the wilderness and came to Horeb, the mountain of God. There the angel of Yahweh appeared to him in the shape of a flame of fire, coming from the middle of a bush. Moses looked; there was the bush blazing but it was not being burnt up. "I must go and look at this strange sight," Moses said "and see why the bush is not burnt." Now Yahweh saw him go forward to look, and God called to him from the middle of the bush. "Moses, Moses!" he said. "Here I am," he answered. "Come no nearer," he said. "Take off your shoes, for the place on which you stand is holy ground. I am the God of our father," he said, "the God of Abraham, the God of Isaac and the God of Jacob." At this Moses covered his face, afraid to look at God. (Exod. 3:1–6)

Is this story too familiar to make us still awestruck? Or can we recover the power of this vision: a bush ablaze, yet unharmed? This is one of the images that has left a lasting impression on the religious mind throughout the ages. In its immediate context, the blazing flame amid the desert bramble stands for the divine Presence among God's people; it stands for "the Holy One of Israel." But in a more general sense the thorn bush burning, yet unburnt, is much more. It is an everyday yet amazing occurrence when, with the eyes of our heart, we see all things aflame with divine fire.

The paradox that shines from the Burning Bush becomes clear only when later prophets translate that image into the formula "the Holy One in the midst of you."

Holiness here does not refer to moral perfection so much as God's unimaginable otherness. The paradox bursts upon us when we encounter that unimaginably other One in the midst of what is most familiar to us. Two attitudes are apt to blind us to that encounter: worldliness and otherworldliness. Worldliness sees merely the bramble; otherworldliness sees merely the fire. But to see, with the eyes of the heart, one in the midst of the other, that is the secret of sacramentality.

The only way we can understand this secret is through our own unique personal encounter with the Burning Bush. Psychology, we have seen, calls these moments of private vision in which reality appears transfigured "peak experiences." We all have had these experiences, though some people are more alert to them than others, or more ready to admit them. Peak experiences are always a gift, a surprise. In a flash the things at hand are seen in a new light that slakes the thirst of our heart for ultimate meaning.

A peak experience is a moment when we "get it all together" as is commonly said. All those rifts and cracks of separation, polarity, alienation that we ordinarily experience are healed in one glance. "Like a saint's vision of beatitude. Like the veil of things as they seem drawn back by an unseen hand. For a second you see.... For a second there is meaning."[1] This is the secret of which you catch sight: everything has meaning. And one glimpse of that secret makes everything whole. The secret is the secret of sacramentality, the mystery that God's life is communicated through all things, just as meaning is communicated through words. The two belong together, meaning and word, God and the world. The two belong together, without confusion, and inseparable: meaning and word, God and the world. "He dwells (all of Him dwells) within the seed of the smallest flower and is not cramped: Deep Heaven is inside Him who is inside the seed and does not distend Him. Blessed be He!"[2] "For a second you see — and seeing the secret, are the secret!"[3] You are the secret because you are seeing it with the eyes of your heart. No other eyes can see it.

For this reason sacramental life always unfolds in community, together. It is never a private affair, though it is deeply personal. Sacramentality is the secret that here on earth, all communicate to all, in a myriad different ways, the life of the Holy One in the midst of us. Our communities are merely pointers toward that one great family of God, more or less successful models and partial realizations of it. Their celebrations of life are somehow sacraments, because life itself is sacramental.

It is hard to imagine someone truly understanding the Lord's Supper, for instance, without having learned to look with the eyes of the heart at the robin gulping down an earthworm to feed her young in the nest. The universal law that life must give its life to feed new life simply mirrors the surpassing mystery that through God's love we have life — God's life — by the very death of God. This mystery of the Eucharist comes into focus whenever a community shares a meal mindfully, gratefully.

Biblical tradition (Jewish, Christian, Islamic) sees with particular clarity that sacramental life is realized in time, in history. This is how the Rabbis put it: unless Moses had been taking care of the sheep, he never would have come upon the Burning Bush. Unless we serve life, in the give and take that this involves on all levels, we shall never discover its sacramental power. That togetherness in which sacramental life is rooted includes the dimensions of time, of history, of struggle, of suffering, of service. Moses not only came upon the Burning Bush in the midst of his daily work as a shepherd, but this vision compelled him to struggle for the liberation of his people.

There is only one condition for seeing life sacramentally: "Take off your shoes!" Realize that the ground on which we stand is holy ground. The act of taking off our shoes is a gesture of thanksgiving, and it is through thanksgiving that we enter into sacramental life. We shouldn't forget the grace received in going barefoot either. Going barefoot actually helps. There is no more immediate way of getting in touch with reality than direct physical contact: to feel the difference between walking on sand, on grass, on smooth granite warmed by the sun, on the forest floor; to let the pebbles hurt us for a while; to squeeze the mud between our toes. There are so many ways of gratefully touching God's healing power through the earth. Whenever we take off the dullness of being-used-to it, of taking things for granted, life in all its freshness touches us and we see that all life is sacramental. If we could measure our aliveness, surely it is the degree to which we are in touch with the Holy One as the inexhaustible fire in the midst of all things.

PART TWO

God,

Religion, and Us

We do not grow up in gardens of Eden. We are born
in a particular point of time and in a particular place.
Early on, we are taught right from wrong as interpreted by
our parents and teachers, our priests or rabbis. They may be
full of love or full of anger — or somewhere in between. We
learn forgiveness from the second chances they give us as well
as from the holy books they read to us. Or we learn to give
up because of one too many bumps or bruises and no helping
hand. All this becomes part of our frame of reference. All this
is woven into who we are as well as the culture and institutions
that express and support our basic values and needs. The more
we understand these influences, the deeper we can dig in our
own search for meaning.

In this second group of essays Brother David untangles the
network of influences that shape our different expressions of

spirituality, including our beliefs about God and the defining characteristics of major religious traditions. What makes these expressions real is the Sacred at the core of each of them. Discovering the Sacred at their core is our challenge, says Brother David. We must be able to distinguish between "faithfulness to life and faithfulness to the structures that life has created in the past." This discernment is an ongoing process. Like every generation of believers, we must be able to recognize "the original light" that is without distortions.

CHAPTER 5

VIEWS OF THE COSMOS

This chapter sets the stage for the second group of essays by looking at our most basic religious experience, our "encounter with Mystery." One way to understand an "encounter with Mystery" is to think about what happens when we look out into the night sky and allow our spirit to wonder. Our openness to — or estrangement from — that which we do not and cannot know affects how we view the world: our expectations and assumptions, what we think we are seeing and what we ignore. When we are fully open, even to the unknowable, we are in touch with the center of our spiritual life.

We are at a unique point in history, Brother David shows in this essay. We have moved beyond the dominance of Greek culture in which Mystery was all but snuffed out as science and technology took center stage. The Greek emphasis on phenomena and its passion for consistency left no room for anything that it could not control. Today, however, we are able to enjoy the compatibility of science and revelation and the picture of the world they give us. It is one that is both "right in perspective and correct in detail." It has opened new frontiers for us to explore Mystery.

If we can acknowledge the endurance of Mystery, then we can truly have vision, Brother David says. And if we can connect the Mystery "out there" to the one in our own center of being, we also can regain a sense of wonder that ancient people once knew: "The staggering possibility that our little life may become ultimately meaningful as a celebration of that Mystery in which it is rooted."

There are two views of the cosmos, which find expression in early myths about the world's origin: an open worldview and a closed worldview.

To the *open worldview* the universe is an immense house, as it were, with transparent walls. But outside, beyond the transparent walls of this house, it is always night. Here is the darkness of Mystery, the invisible presence of the utterly Other, nameless, imageless.

As humans try to understand this mystery in which their world is embedded, they naturally begin to project images of what is invisible to them onto these walls. Eventually, however, the walls turn out to hide more than they reveal and a *closed worldview* emerges. The darkness of human loneliness and estrangement in the world becomes filled with dreams. Humans can become so preoccupied with the dream images their own minds project that they lose the power of looking through at the night. The transparent walls of their cosmic house become opaque and finally a closed worldview denies that any mystery at all could lie beyond.

As we study the worldview of ancient peoples, going as far back as we can in history and prehistory, the picture of earliest religion stands in sharp contrast to the preconceived ideas that eighteenth- and nineteenth-century anthropologists assumed to be true. They simply took it for granted that all religious notions and the human mind in general must have developed step by step in close parallel to physiological evolution, i.e., from a "savage" stage to ever greater refinement. During the twentieth century, however, a wealth of objective material accumulated that proves that the most ancient cultural stratum to which we can penetrate by anthropological methods is simple but by no means "savage."

One remarkable feature of the oldest known religious beliefs is the notion of a Supreme Being who is beyond the world, in no way part of the cosmos, but often said to be its maker and sustainer. Sometimes the way in which this Supreme Being made the world is described in elaborate myths; sometimes only the fact of creation is stated, as when the Baining people of New Britain say: "He brought all things into being by inexplicable ways." Frequently the Supreme Being is described as making the world by thinking it, by a word or command, by singing or by merely wishing it to be. The Wijot in northern California, for example, say: "The Old Man Above did not use earth and sticks to make men. He simply thought, and there they were."

At this point we must remind ourselves that a creation myth, though cast in the form of a historic account, is basically a metaphysical statement. It is a story in answer to a question: What happened in the beginning? But "the beginning" in this context is a temporal expression for an ontological insight. When the child or the childlike mind of the mythmaker asks what happened before, always this question concerns the link between all that is and the source of it all. It seems to be more difficult for the adult mind than it is for the child to intuit that the

Source of all there is cannot possibly be an additional something. It is Mystery.

Filled with wonderment like a true philosopher, the child says: "The world is so you have something to stand on." Or "A floor is so you don't fall into the hole your house is in." This is what it means to see the world against the background of mystery. What really counts for the child and the mythmaker is the relationship of things to that background. That is the real concern of a creation myth.

One of the most charming and profound statements about this relationship is embodied in a creation myth by the Jicarilla Apache of New Mexico:

> Dog was going around with Creator. Everywhere he went, Dog went, and watched all that he did. When Creator finished one job and moved on to another, the dog went too.
>
> "Are you going to stay around here all the time?" said the dog. "Or will you have to go away?"
>
> "Well, perhaps someday I shall have to live far away," said Creator.
>
> "Then, Grandfather, will you make me a companion?" So Creator lay down on the ground.
>
> "Draw a line around me with your paw," he said.
>
> So Dog scratched an outline in the earth all around the great Creator. Creator got up and looked at it.
>
> "Go a little way off and don't look," he said. The dog went off a little way. In a few minutes he looked.
>
> "Oh, someone is lying where you were lying, Grandfather."

"Go along and don't look," said Creator. The dog went a little farther. In a few minutes he looked.

"Someone is sitting there, Grandfather," he said.

"Turn around and walk farther off," said Creator. The dog obeyed.

At last Creator called the dog. "Now you can look," he said.

"Oh, Grandfather, he moves," cried the dog in delight.

So they stood by the man and looked him over. "Pretty good," said Creator.

"He's wonderful," said the dog.

Creator went behind the man and lifted him to his feet.

"Put out your foot," he said. "Walk. Do this." So the man walked.

"Now run," said Creator. But the man said nothing.

Four times Creator told the man to talk. "Say words," he said. Finally the man said words. He spoke.

"Now shout," said Creator. He gave a big yell himself and showed the man how.

The man shouted.

"What else?" he said.

Creator thought a minute.

"Laugh," he said. "Laugh, laugh, laugh, laugh." Then the man laughed.

The dog was very happy when the man laughed. He jumped up on him and ran off a little, and ran back and jumped up on him. He kept jumping up

69

on him the way dogs do today when they are full of
love and delight.
   The man laughed and laughed.
   "Now you are fit to live," said Creator.
   So the man went off with his dog.[1]

I selected this particular myth for three reasons: it is one of my favorites, it exemplifies the open worldview with great clarity, and it hints already at the threat of a gradually closing worldview. What makes the central image so unique in this myth is its subtlety: the origin of human life is connected with its mysterious source by an empty outline, an outline drawn on the ground by an animal's paw, yet mysteriously containing the master mind of all there is — for that is what the Creator stands for.

Will this Creator always be near? No, perhaps some day he will have to live far away. Will have to? Yes, because the man went off with his dog. If we listen attentively, we perceive a deep sorrow in this myth about the creation of laughter. It is a fine but firm bond that links laughter and sorrow. That only we humans can laugh stems from the fact that only we are capable of a sorrow, a grief too deep for words. People tell each other about their little pains. About their great sorrows they are silent. All the myth tells us is that "the man went off with his dog" — eloquently silent about this alienation from Mystery.

The anthropological data agree with this poetic vision: the Supreme Being is pushed into the background as people become more and more preoccupied with "deities associated with their daily needs, that is, with the minor gods. The Supreme Being thus develops into what has been admirably described as an otiose deity, one resting on his laurels after the creation of the world and leaving it entirely to its own devices."[2]

"When his work was done, he disappeared," say the Pomo Indians of California. "Hold together," he told the world, for the last time, and disappeared.[3]

In other myths estrangement from the Supreme Being is explained by a misunderstanding, by human disobedience, or by some fatal coincidence. Often death and sickness and all human misery are said to result from this estrangement, sometimes as a punishment. But whatever the cause of the estrangement, it sheds a new light on the world. Now the human mind perceives the world in the light of this estrangement. Or shall we call it the "darkness" of estrangement? It is a darkness filled with dreams. At first this worldview remains "open" toward that which lies beyond the cosmos. But this Beyond is the altogether Other, the great and painful Question raised by everything around us, cross-questioning a person's innermost heart as he or she "walks off with his [or her] dog."

In connection with creation myths, the more ancient concept of a Supreme Being persists even in a more complex cultural environment, at least in the form of one supreme head of a hierarchy or family of gods. But these minor gods are much closer to human concerns than the transcendent Creator, who made both humans and the gods. For they are personifications of the powers that most preoccupy people in daily life, especially in agrarian cultures: the earth, vegetation, sun, moon, stars, seasons, the weather. Sometimes they are magnified figures of ancestors. The more their characteristics are projected onto the image of the Supreme Being, the more the concept of creation changes from a "making" to a "begetting" of the world by the gods, or to an impersonal evolving of both gods and world out of primordial chaos. Where this process is completed, people no longer take the transcendent into view. Their worldview becomes a "closed" one.

It has not always been sufficiently stressed that the open and the closed worldview are two diametrically opposed metaphysical perspectives. Yet we must also stress a psychological similarity, in spite of their metaphysical opposition. Metaphysically the Mystery on which the open worldview focuses is altogether transcendent, although it will not be neatly distinguished in every case from mysterious phenomena that belong to the cosmos. For the closed worldview, on the other hand, there is nothing beyond this cosmos, nothing transcendent, and so mystery is merely that which lies beyond peoples' comprehension. But psychologically, Mystery is in both cases the "real reality" behind everything; in both cases it is known through symbol, expressed through myth and shared through ritual. Myth, symbol, and ritual are the forms of humanity's encounter with Mystery, and so they will bear the marks of this encounter, which has one kind of emphasis within the framework of the open view of the cosmos and quite a different one within the framework of the closed.

Encounter with Mystery is our basic religious experience; it is our confrontation — our coming face to face — with the "Holy," with a power beyond our comprehension which challenges us, and to which we yet feel akin. This experience places us humans at the crossroads of two tendencies: the tendency to give ourselves over to this power (the religious attitude toward the Holy), and the tendency to lay hold of this power, to make use of it according to our own will (the magic attitude toward the Holy). Most often we find both tendencies expressed side by side in primordial no less than in contemporary religion.

The religious attitude will be emphasized to the extent to which a person's world is "transparent" for the transcendent. This stands to reason. For the only appropriate attitude toward the "All-powerful," the "Unexplainable," is reverence and obedience.

We can become aware of reaching the center of the universe, the mythic point of contact with transcendence, whenever we return to our own inmost heart. There, at the very core of our being, we encounter the nearness of that Mystery, which surrounds all things beyond the farthest horizon. In discovering this polarity of center and periphery, we discover our own life as the Cosmic Tree springing up from the taproot of creation and branching out into a region beyond space and time. We discover Mystery at the center of our own heart and sense the staggering possibility that our little life may become ultimately meaningful as celebration of that Mystery in which it is rooted.

Ritual brings us to this center. For the open worldview, this center is the point at which the cosmos is open toward the trans-cosmic. Symbol is the static expression of this openness, ritual the dynamic one. The function of ritual is to bring a person to this center, to this point of communication. The ritual center becomes the place of meeting as ritual brings about the moment of encounter. Through ritual, space is open toward that which is beyond space; time is open toward that which is beyond time.

To understand the modern worldview, we need to explore its origin in Greek thought where there is no "beyond" from which light could come. Myth, symbol, and ritual of this opaque world could not be transformed; they were bound to be destroyed. "Man does not worship what he thinks he can control,"[4] and when, through the intellectual adventure of the Greek mind, science and technology evolved, people could begin to hope that they would gain control over cosmic powers. That there are no other powers was tacitly taken for granted.

We shall see how important this assumption became in the course of a development that has already lasted twenty-five centuries. Only in recent times was this development enormously broadened and accentuated through the use of scientific experimentation and the use of modern technology. But in seed it was all prepared from the moment the Greek philosophers began to approach mystery reflexively, no longer taking it for granted as children do, but approaching it with the skepticism typical of adolescence.

Like a child, "early man was confronted not by an inanimate, impersonal nature — not by an 'It,' but a 'Thou....' Such a relationship involved not only man's intellect but the whole of his being — his feeling and his will, no less than his thought. Hence early man would have rejected the detachment of a purely intellectual attitude toward nature, had he been able to conceive it, as inadequate to his experience."[5] But among the Greek philosophers contemporary with the Hebrew prophets, this purely intellectual approach breaks through as a new power, a power destined to shape the world with ever increasing impetus. One of the leading physicists of our time, Erwin Schroedinger, borrows a phrase from John Burnet and describes science simply as "thinking about the world in the Greek way."

This Greek way of looking at the cosmos is characterized above all by its preoccupation with the world of phenomena, by its power of abstraction, and by a passion for consistency. These three factors operate within the framework of the closed worldview and are in some way its expression, because each one of them implies an important restriction of vision. The preoccupation with the phenomenal world cuts out meaning and purpose in order to focus sharply on observable facts alone, oscillating, however, from the beginning between the extremes of taking them for the only reality (Democritus) and denying them reality altogether (Parmenides). Abstraction becomes objectivity and tries to cut out as far as possible the human observer. And the Greek passion for consistency, finding its expression in "the hypothesis that the display of nature can be understood"[6] and predicted, must, at least for methodical reasons, eliminate Mystery, the Unpredictable. We can easily see that there is no room for myth, symbol, and ritual in this world of mere science.

"Mythos," in its original sense, means a statement of ultimate truth accepted on the authority of tradition; "Logos," in contrast, meant originally a statement of truth derived from discursive reasoning. And this discursive reasoning now replaces tradition as the only valid authority. Myth is replaced by logic. The "symbols" with which this logic manipulates are not symbols in the sense in which we have been using the term. Here the dimension of mystery in which things partake, thereby becoming symbols in our sense, must be excluded from consideration in order to make terms manageable within an exclusively intellectual frame of reference. What used to be a whole "thing with meaning" is now split up into observable facts and abstract terms. These are the realities that count within this frame of reference. And since ritual is the means of one's participation in that reality which ultimately counts for him or her, the new "ritual" must be logical speculation and scientific experimentation.

When the Greeks, looking at the cosmos, asked for the "origin," what they sought was not understood in the terms of myth; they asked for an immanent and lasting ground of existence. For the first time the universe was conceived as an intelligible whole without reference to any transcendent reality. It is intelligible because human beings can comprehend the cosmic order. Heraclitus asserted that the universe was intelligible because it was ruled by "thought" or "judgment" (Logos) and the same principle, therefore, governed both existence and Knowledge.[7]

It is important to note that the essence of this Logos concept is not an optional superstructure but the very foundation stone for "the Greek way of thinking about the world." Unless a unifying principle gave order to the cosmos, and unless a person could grasp this principle and thus in part, at least, comprehend that order, all science would break down.

Have we thus found an inner cosmic light to make the world meaningful for us without reference to Mystery? Heraclitus makes a statement that seems to express as closed a worldview as one could imagine: "This ordered world, which is the same for all, not one of the gods or men has made; but it was ever, is now, and ever shall be an ever-living fire, flaring up according to measure and going out according to measure." The measure of its flaring up and its going out is determined by the Logos that brings forth harmony from the tension of opposites "as in a bow or in a lyre."

All seems self-contained. And yet this is the point where the Greek worldview does remain open after all. For, by definition, the human mind has a share in the Logos. And the Logos is unfathomable. Our mind, that "clearest-selved spark"[8] of the Logos fire, is dark unto itself; it cannot sound out its own depth.

We have Heraclitus's own word for it: "the soul's frontiers you could not find in your wandering, though you traveled every road: so deep is its Logos." The human heart communicates with the mystery in which the universe is embedded, like those inland lakes that communicate underground with the ocean. We can comprehend the sustaining principle of cosmic order, but only as pointing beyond itself toward mystery. The fire of Heraclitus, the Dark One, as they called him, is a dark fire.

Should we consider it mere coincidence that Hebrew prophets proclaimed the Great Sunrise on a transparent world at the very hour at which Greek thinkers destroyed the mirror world of the closed worldview? Thales of Miletus, who says that "all things are full of gods," but goes ahead and treats them as mere things, implicitly agrees with the psalmist who sings: "All the gods of heathens are nothings." Of course the psalmist adds: "but the Lord made the heavens" (Ps. 95:5). The "lesser gods" who are part of the cosmos may one by one be dethroned as scientific knowledge of the universe expands. The

Transcendent One will not be affected; he lives beyond Olympus. If the Greek way of looking at the world gradually removed myth, symbol, and ritual from the closed world, biblical religion merely remarks that what could be destroyed in them had never been worth preserving. The perennial roots of myth, symbol, and ritual cannot be destroyed. For we can never settle down to live content side by side with the unknown. Sooner or later we will rise to face it. And as long as anything remains unknown, the Unknowable has not been completely ruled out; mystery (the unknown) implicitly points toward Mystery (the Unknowable).

Does this not imply that the further we discover the world, the more magnificently will the frontier expand at which we meet God? Indeed, not only will there be more points of contact, as it were, but there will be new and deeper vistas. As far as the biblical view of the cosmos is concerned, revelation merely opens our eyes to the light. Only through living, loving contact with the things around us will we actually see. And science is one form of this contact with the world, a limited one, that is true, but one of great importance. Through their transformation by the pre-Socratic philosophers and the Hebrew prophets the two worldviews became compatible and complementary. Only together do revelation and science give us a concept of the world that is both right in perspective and correct in detail.

One might smile at this optimistic approach, or even get angry and point out the clashes in the past. But we shall not be able to make a true and full view of the cosmos our own unless we realize that these clashes were not at all between revelation and science. How can science, which never claims to explore anything but this universe, clash with the revelation of that which lies beyond? The clashes of the past were never between science and dogma (i.e., the necessary and legitimate formulation of revelation), but between scientism and dogmatism. Scientism, which restricts humanity's whole worldview to the limited perspective of science, and dogmatism, which makes the world image of a certain period in history an absolute — these two must clash. And the deadlock between them is one cause of humankind's present dilemma.

Science, as we saw, happened to grow up in an environment with a closed worldview. That is why from the beginning scientism grew up along with it. The gods of Greece, personifications of natural forces and of human desires, must necessarily totter and fall before a new way of looking at the cosmos. But beyond Olympus the Greeks knew no transcendent heaven. Was it not logical, then, to extend the approach of science to the whole of life? This was all the more alluring as it made humanity "the measure of all things." To retain the illusion of being the absolute, human beings must of course keep their eyes closed as best they can to that which by definition transcends their comprehension. One can hardly call that an outlook; but for lack of a better term let us call it the profane outlook on life, the negative extreme of the closed worldview.

Just as scientism grew up with true science, so dogmatism with true dogma. And just as scientism is but one symptom of the profane outlook, so dogmatism is but one symptom of what I would like to call "domesticated religion." Myth is the proclamation of mystery;

but domesticated religion cuts mystery to size and reduces it to dogmatism; it keeps mystery at arm's length by turning religion into a social convention. Symbols call for awe; but domesticated religion thinks it can "manage" mystery through a "sacramental automatism" that approaches magic and is, of course, a perversion of the Catholic concept of sacrament. Domesticated religion perverts myth, symbol, and ritual by turning the personal reality of Mystery into an object. The profane outlook denies the existence of Mystery altogether, and so leaves no room for myth, symbol, and ritual. Thus neither the one nor the other can attain to a worldview in any true sense. There can be no vision without acceptance of Mystery.

CHAPTER 6

THE MYSTICAL CORE OF ORGANIZED RELIGION

Religion is inevitable, Brother David tells us. This is because we do with our mystical experiences what human beings do with every experience. We analyze them. We form opinions either for or against them. And we try to hold on to and celebrate what is good. Each of these responses is a starting point for the doctrines, moral codes, and rituals that are a part of every organized religion.

This essay traces religion back to its mystical beginnings and back to our own search for meaning. Only in this interconnection can religion do what it is meant to do: keep us faithful as well as set us free; center us and propel us to new dimensions. But, as Brother David is well aware, this is never a self-sustaining process. In the unavoidable refraction of the Truth, Beauty, and Goodness at the heart of sacred traditions is the potential for religious institutions to encumber, not support, life. Doctrine can quickly deteriorate into dogmatism, the ethical moral codes that are part of every religion can turn into moralism, and our sacred rituals can become ritualism.

We can't be bystanders in religion, complacent recipients of the law, Brother David shows. We must challenge and question, and we must reclaim and sustain the original spirit of our faith. Only then can "the heart of religion find itself in the religion of the heart."

The discovery of mysticism as everyone's inalienable right brings with it a puzzling tension, and those who feel this tension most keenly are people who have long been members of an established religion. They may have discovered the mystical reality inside the religious establishment or outside of it: either in church or on a mountaintop, while listening to Bach's B-Minor Mass, or while watching a sunset. In any case, those who taste mystical ecstasy — especially out in nature — may begin to sense a discrepancy between this undeniably religious experience and the "forms" that normally pass as religious.

If we accept that our religious pursuits are essentially the human quest for meaning and that mysticism is the experience of communion with Ultimate Reality (with "God," if you feel comfortable with this time-honored name), then mystical experiences are not only "religious," they are, in fact, the very heart of religion. Yet the body of religion doesn't always accept its heart. To the establishment, mysticism is suspect. Why become absorbed in the *Cloud of Unknowing* when the establishment spells everything out so clearly? And isn't an emphasis on personal experience a bit egocentric? Who can be sure that people standing on their own feet won't go their own way? These suspicions gave rise to the famous saying that "myst-i-cism begins with mist, puts the I in the center, and ends in schism."

This tension between the mystic and the religious establishment exists in every religion, Eastern or Western. As the great mystic Rumi (1207–73), who attacked his own Muslim establishment, said, "When the school and the mosque and the minaret get torn down, then the dervishes can begin their community."[1] Al Hallaj (c. 858–922), on the other hand, was attacked by that same establishment, tortured, and crucified for his mystical lifestyle and convictions, a persecution not without political overtones.

One way or the other, the same plot is acted out repeatedly throughout history. Every religion seems to begin with mysticism and end up in politics. If we could understand the inner workings of this process, maybe we could deal with the tension between mystical religion and religious establishment in a new way. Maybe we could transform the polarization into a mutually vitalizing polarity. Understanding would certainly make us more compassionate with those caught up on both sides of the struggle.

The question we need to tackle is this: How does one get from mystical experience to an established religion? My one-word answer is: inevitably. What makes the process inevitable is that we do with our mystical experience what we do with every experience: we try to understand it; we opt for or against it; we express our feelings with regard to it. Do this with your mystical experience and you have all the makings of a religion.

Moment by moment, throughout all our experiences, our *intellect* keeps in step, interpreting what we perceive. This is especially true when we have one of those deeply meaningful moments. Our intellect swoops down upon these mystical experiences and starts its analysis. Religious *doctrine* begins at precisely this point. No religion in the world can exist without a doctrine. And there is no religious doctrine that could not ultimately be traced back to mystical experience, however long and entangled those roots are likely to be. Even if you claim for yourself a "private" religion with no doctrine or "a deep religious awareness that cannot be put into words," that would be an example of exactly what we are talking about: an intellectual interpretation of your experience. Your "doctrine" would be a piece of so-called negative (apophatic) theology found in most religions, which expresses knowledge of the Divine by describing what it is not.

Forming an opinion is not all we do. On the basis of that opinion, we take sides for or against; we desire or reject. This is where our *will* comes into play. As soon as we recognize something as good for us, we cannot help desiring it. We commit ourselves willingly to go after what we desire. The moment we taste the mystical bliss of universal belonging, we say a willing yes to it. In this unconditional yes lies the root of *ethics,* that is, in essence, acting toward everyone as one acts when one feels a sense of belonging.

If the intellect sifts out what is true and the will reaches out for what is good, there is also a third dimension to reality: beauty. Our whole being resonates with what is beautiful, like a crystal lampshade that reverberates every time you hit a C-sharp on the piano. When this feeling of resonance (or, in other situations, dissonance) marks our interaction with the world, we speak of the *emotions.* Joyfully our emotions reverberate with the beauty of our mystical experience. The more engaged we are emotionally in this experience, the more we will celebrate its uplift. We may remember the day and the hour and celebrate it year after year. We may go back to the garden bench where we heard the singing of the thrush that deepened our sense of connection with not only this bird but all of nature. We may never hear the bird again, but we have created a *ritual,* a kind of pilgrimage undertaken to a personal holy place. Ritual is an element of every religion. Every ritual in the world celebrates belonging in one form or another, pointing toward that ultimate belonging we experience in moments of mystical awareness.

The response we give in those moments is always wholehearted. In the heart, at the core of the human person, intellect, will, and emotions still form an integral whole. Yet — and this is critical to recognize — once the response of the heart expresses itself in thinking, willing, or feeling, the original wholeness of the response is refracted or broken. That is why we are never fully satisfied with the expression of those deepest insights in word or image. Nor is our willing commitment to justice and peace, our yes to belonging, as wholehearted on the practical level as it is in moments of mystical communion. Similarly, our feelings are not sustained, and we often fail to celebrate the beauty that we glimpsed unveiled for a moment and that continues to shine through the veil of daily reality.

It is in this sense that doctrine, ethics, and ritual bear the mark of our shortcomings, even in the earliest buds of religion. At the same time, they fulfill an important function: they keep us connected, no matter how imperfectly, with the truth, goodness, and beauty that once overwhelmed us. That is the glory of every religion.

Doctrine, ethics, and ritual generally work like an irrigation system, which is meant to bring ever fresh water from the source of mysticism into daily life. These irrigation systems differ from one religion to another. Some are simply more efficient. But subjective preferences are also important. We are comfortable with the familiar. No matter what other models may be on the market, the one we are used to seems more effective. But time also has an influence on the system: pipes get rusty and start to leak, or they get clogged. The flow from the source slows down to a trickle.

Fortunately, these systems maintain some level of effectiveness. Unfortunately, deterioration begins on the day the system is installed. At first, doctrine is simply the interpretation of mystical reality; it flows from it and leads back to it. But then the intellect begins to interpret that interpretation. Commentaries on commentaries are piled on top of the original doctrine. With every new interpretation of the previous one, we move farther away from the experiential source. Live doctrine fossilizes into dogmatism.

A similar process inevitably takes place with ethics. At first, moral precepts simply spell out how to translate mystical communion into practical living. The precepts remind us to act as one acts among people who belong together, and so they keep pointing back to our deepest, mystical sense of belonging. (The fact that a community will often draw too narrow a circle around itself is a different matter. That's simply an inadequate translation of the original intuition. The circle of mystical communion is all-inclusive.) But in our desire to express unwavering commitment to the goodness we glimpsed in mystical moments, we engrave the moral precepts on stone tablets. In doing so, we render the expression of that commitment unchangeable. Stone-engraved, these expressions are unable to reflect changing circumstances that call for a different expression of the same commitment. As the do's and don'ts become static, morality turns into moralism.

What happens with ritual? At first, it is a true celebration. We remember gratefully those moments in which we were most deeply aware of limitless belonging. Everything else besides this awareness is optional. As a reminder and renewal of our ultimate connectedness, the celebration has religious overtones that echo mystical communion. This is why, when we celebrate, we want all those who belong to us in a special way to be present. Repetition also is a part of celebration. Every time we celebrate a birthday, for example, that day is enriched by memory upon memory of all previous ones. But repetition has its dangers, especially for the celebration of religious rituals. Because they are so important, we strive to perfect the ritual, and before we know it, we are more concerned with form than with content. When form becomes formalized and content is forgotten, ritual turns into ritualism.

The figure on the following page is an attempt to depict this process (and its happy ending, when all goes well). The arrows represent the flow of mystical light, as it were. The white light of original wholeness is refracted through the lens of the mind's action (the Founder's own mind to begin with). As intellect, will, and emotions inevitably process the mystical experience, the basic elements of religion (doctrine, ethics, ritual) originate. Religion in its diverse expressions is now filtered through historical influence (e.g., institutionalization) and tends to deteriorate. It can, however, be purified and renewed whenever a faithful heart recognizes, in spite of all distortions, the original light. Thus, the believer's mysticism becomes one with the Founder's. The heart of religion finds itself in the religion of the heart. The two are one.

The Movement from Founder's Mysticism to Believer's Mysticism

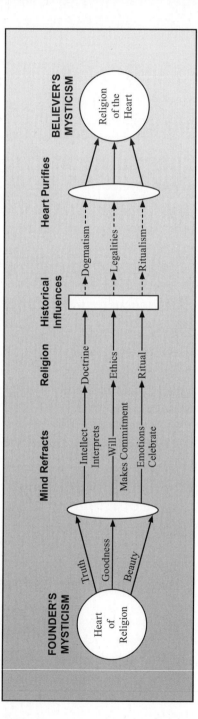

Sad as it is, religion left to itself — without the mystic in each of us to renew it — turns irreligious. Once, in Hawaii, after I had been walking on still-hot volcanic rock, an image for this process occurred to me: the image of fire. The beginnings of the great religions were like the eruptions of a volcano. There was fire, there was heat, there was light: the light of mystical insight, freshly spelled out in a new teaching; the best of hearts aglow with commitment to a sharing community; and celebration, as fiery as new wine.

The light of doctrine, the glow of ethical commitment, and the fire of ritual celebration were expressions that gushed forth red hot from the depths of mystical consciousness. But as that stream of lava flowed down the sides of the mountain, it began to cool off. The farther it got from its origins, the less it looked like fire; it turned into rock. Dogmatism, moralism, ritualism: all are layers of ash deposits and volcanic rock that separate us from the fiery magma deep down below.

But there are fissures and clefts in the igneous rock of the old lava flows; there are hot springs, fumaroles, and geysers; there are even occasional earthquakes and minor eruptions. These represent the great men and women who reformed and renewed religious tradition from within. In one way or another, this is our task, too. Every religion has a mystical core. The challenge is to find access to it and to live in its power. In this sense, every generation of believers is challenged anew to make its religion truly religious.

This is the point where mysticism clashes with the institution. We need religious institutions. If they weren't there, we would create them. Life creates structures. Think of the ingenious constructions life invents to protect its seeds, of all those husks and hulls and pods, the shucks and burrs and capsules found in an autumn hedgerow. Come spring, the new life within cracks these containers (even walnut shells!) and bursts forth. Crust, rind, and chaff split open and are discarded. Our social structures, however, have a tendency to perpetuate themselves. Religious institutions are less likely than seed pods to yield to the new life stirring within. And although life (over and over again) creates structures, structures do not create life.

Those who are closest to the life that created the structures will have the greatest respect for them; they will also be the first ones, however, to demand that structures that no longer support but encumber life be changed. Closest to the mystical core of religion, they will often be uncomfortable agitators within the system. How genuine they are will show itself by their compassionate understanding for those whom they must oppose; after all, mystics come from a realm where "we" and "they" are one.

In some cases, officials of institutional religion are themselves mystics, as was true of Pope John XXIII. These are the men and women who sense when the time has come for the structures to yield to life. They can distinguish between faithfulness to life and faithfulness to the structures that life has created in the past, and they get their priorities right. Rumi did so when he wrote:

> Not until faithfulness turns into betrayal
> and betrayal into faith
> can any human being become part of truth.[2]

Note that betrayal — or what is seen as such — is not the last step; there is a further one, in which betrayal turns into faith. This going out and returning is the journey of the hero; it is our task. Faith (i.e., courageous trust) lets go of institutional structures and so finds them on a higher level — again and again. This process is as painful as life, and equally surprising.

One of the great surprises is that the fire of mysticism can melt even the rigor mortis of dogmatism, legalism, and ritualism. By the glance or the touch of those whose hearts are burning, doctrine, ethics, and ritual come aglow with the truth, goodness, and beauty of the original fire. The dead letter comes alive, breathing freedom. "God's writing engraved on the tablets" is what the uninitiated reads in Exodus 32:16. But only the consonants are written in the Hebrew text: (*chrth*). Mystics who happen to be rabbis look at this word and say: Don't read *charath* (engraved); read *cheruth* (freedom)! God's writing is not "engraved"; it is freedom!

CHAPTER 7

THE GOD PROBLEM

Can we get beyond preconceived notions of a God who divides believers or stirs up negative feelings like guilt and skepticism? What if instead we follow the advice of Jesus and rely on the inner authority that resides within each of us, and by which we can recognize true ultimate authority? What if we allow ourselves to be quiet and open enough to discover for ourselves that which we know is true?

Returning to the theme of our "peak experiences," this essay explores the God-view that mystics have always known. It is through our own mystical experiences, Brother David shows, that we can know a God who heals and unifies, who is transcendent but not separate, beyond but not above. It is in our own experiences that we can find a Presence strong enough to affect how we live and how we relate to one another. Belonging is fundamental to the kingdom of this God.

Relying on what Brother David calls our own "spiritual backbone" will also help us to recognize different aspects of the More in each of the major religious traditions. Taken together, he says, they reflect the true meaning of Trinity: God is in all and all is in God.

Spiritual health depends on your God-view, and it's no surprise that a growing body of research suggests that spiritual health and physical health are deeply intertwined. "Spirit," as we have seen, is Latin for "life-breath," and spirituality is aliveness — super-aliveness. We may think of it as the highest frequency of life power, even while the whole bandwidth of life oscillates as one. If we stay with this image, we may envisage our relationship to Ultimate Reality — to God, if you want — as the grounding of the life-current.

The idea of "grounding" is where spirituality connects with religion. The goal of religion is to reestablish broken bonds to our deepest self, to society and nature, and to the very Ground of Being. Religion ties us again to our own depth, which is one with the fathomless depth from which the whole universe wells up. This broad sense of Religion (capital "R") is the shared mystical matrix of the world's various religions (small "r"), the spiritual humus from which these religions sprout in all their diversity.

Strangely, however, the prevailing notion of God in our culture stresses not grounding in the divine matrix, but rather separation. God is seen as an all-powerful Super-Someone over against us. "He" (and it's vital at this point to acknowledge how the idea of God as male haunts many feminists who oppose it) is somehow "over there," and we are "over here." Between God and us humans — between God and everything else, for that matter — gapes an existential gap. God's very holiness is understood as separateness. All other aspects of our culture's God-view are determined by this basic conviction that God is absolutely other and separate. Rather than being grounded, our spiritual wires are left dangling.

Keenly uncomfortable with this gap, an ever-increasing number of people are challenging the dominant God-view on the basis of their own inner God-awareness. Jesus did so in his time. Based on the inner authority of his mystic awareness, he stood up to outer authority. But many of his followers missed the point. Instead of relying on their inner authority, as he had encouraged them to do, they turned Jesus into the new external authority. The time was not ripe. Al Hallaj the Moslem, Spinoza the Jew, and countless others throughout the centuries also challenged the God-view of their time on the strength of their inner conviction. Once this process is set in motion, it gains momentum, and, I believe, it cannot be stopped.

Something comparable happened in biological evolution from an outer skeleton to an inner one. A crab gets its stability from without by its shell; a human's support comes from the spine within. Spiritually, a similar evolutionary leap is happening today. If the crusty shell you have worn since you were first told about God is now cracking, feel your spine. Have you ever seen a turned-over beetle struggling in vain to get back on its feet? Beetles get their clumsy support from their outer shell. You, having a spiritual spine, can get up and dance.

How can we find our spiritual backbones? One answer to this mystical question takes us again to the realm of psychology (see chapter 2). In the mid-twentieth century, Abraham Maslow was surprised to find that a doctorate in psychology gave him no answer to the question, "What is it that makes us psychologically healthy?" Psychologists had been focused on mental illness, and Maslow's question about mental *health* led him to a discovery as decisive for the emerging God-view as the discoveries of Einstein, Planck, and Heisenberg became for our worldview. He learned that people with outstanding creativity, inner strength, and resilience have one characteristic in common: mystical experiences. Since this term did not fit well into psychological jargon, Maslow soon replaced it with the now-familiar term "peak experiences." He found that our psychological health differs depending on the degree to which we integrate these experiences — and the mystical awareness they bring — into daily living.

Such experiences, as we have seen, can make you snap out of your narrow mental frame of mind. For a moment, at least, fear disappears. You are aware that the universe is of one piece and that you are part of it. This unity of all with all gives deep meaning to all. You experience "a sense of the sacred glimpsed *in* and *through* the particular instance of the present moment." Or, as Maslow puts it in a metaphor, you visit "heaven" — a heaven "which exists all the time, all around us, always available to step into for a little while at least." The essence of this "heaven" is limitless belonging. "In Peak Experiences, the dichotomies, polarities, and conflicts of life tend to be transcended or resolved," Maslow continues. We are where we belong: at peace, at home. It is no wonder that, for millennia, different spiritual traditions have cultivated practices to catapult the dividing mind into wholeness, holiness, and health. Among the best known are Zen, Vipassana, Transcendental Meditation, and Yoga. Centering Prayer is another, building on the age-old Prayer of Silence practiced by Christian mystics.

Peak experiences give us a glimpse of the God-view that can lead to a full and fulfilled life through dedicated practice. It is up to you to create that mystic life for which your background, experience, and talents have uniquely prepared you. And what would it look like? Many perceive the peak experience as a direct encounter with Truth,

Goodness, Beauty, Integrity, Simplicity. As such, these experiences give rise to the guiding values of your life. It will be a life determined by that deep sense of belonging which softens the rigid boundaries of our small ego and liberates us to experience our oneness with all — with all there is, and with the transcendent "More" beyond all.

Mystics, we said, experience a transcendent "More" that goes beyond all there is. Religious authorities tend to interpret this "beyond" as "above," "transcendent" as "separate," and "More" as "more powerful" in an authoritarian sense. Thus, the God-drenched experience of the mystic becomes distorted into the image of an all-powerful divine potentate, ruling the world from above: the absolutely separate God.

Nowhere does this God image become more poisonous than in the resulting notion of sin. The authoritarian view of sin gives it a legal twist and a private focus: the little ego is arraigned before the Judge of the World. But we need not view sin this way. Instead, we need to find a systemic focus and see sin as alienation. We are alienated from Nature, from one another, from ourselves. While this has led us to the brink of global catastrophe, we are free to see alienation as a "not yet" in the birth process of a whole, holy, and healthy cosmos.

We catch a glimpse of this potential in our mystical moments. In a peak experience, "the world is accepted," Maslow points out. "Evil itself is accepted." This does not mean evil is condoned or domesticated. It is "seen in its proper place in the whole." The mystic Dame Julian of Norwich writes, "Sin is behovely [useful]. And all shall be well; and all manner of things shall be well."

This systemic focus brings us beyond individual concerns. In this world in which everything hangs together with everything, nothing is a private affair, not even our own health. More and more people are becoming aware that a toxic environment can cause harm to our bodies. But the process works both ways. The environment can also heal. What helps society grow healthier will affect the personal health of its members. Healing must start with a society's worldview and its deepest layer, the God-view.

Jesus provides a helpful illustration of how a society can be healed by transforming its God-view. I will restrict myself here to four facts universally admitted by scholars who study Jesus as a historical figure. He was a healer; he called God "Abba"; he proclaimed a new social order, which he called "the kingdom of God"; and he taught in parables. These bare historic facts, more basic than all doctrinal speculations, suffice to show that Jesus the healer was mystic, social agitator, and religious reformer. His God-view flowed from his mystic experience and into his vision of a healthy society, reaching individuals as healing power.

"Abba" as a way of addressing God was rare before Jesus. It expresses an intimacy that the English word "Father" fails to convey; "Daddy" comes closer. The Hebrew Bible's predominant notion of God as King of the Universe — whose holiness means absolute Otherness — found expression in the religious attitude of the Pharisees among Jesus' contemporaries. They strove for holiness by separating themselves from persons, things, and situations labeled unclean. Purity was their goal. Jesus, in contrast, picks up a minor, mystical trend of the same biblical tradition. Here the intimate nearness of God determines the God-view, and compassion — rather than purity — becomes the spiritual path.

The Pharisees' striving for purity was socially divisive. Only the well-to-do could afford to follow its meticulous standards; the unwashed masses of the poor were excluded. Jesus challenged this social order of exclusion by one of all-inclusive compassion. This found expression in his shocking table fellowship with social outcasts. The kingdom of God that Jesus thus inaugurated is a society healed from its rifts: clean and unclean, poor and rich, "righteous" and "sinners" are all embraced by God's unconditional love. And not humans only: the birds of the air and the lilies of the field — all of Nature is included.

This sense of belonging is in itself healing. Should it surprise us that faith in this new worldview made the blind see, or that trust in this good news made the deaf hear? More often still, the Gospels record that Jesus healed the lame, empowering them to stand on their own feet, which was a metaphor for a new view of authority.

Authoritarians have a vested interest in a monarchical God at the top of a pyramid of power in that they jockey for position. The healing that Jesus' hearers experienced had its roots in communion with God in their own hearts. Those whose approach to healing is radical — which means "from the roots up" — will always be branded as radicals. Yet an approach that does not start at the roots by healing a poisonous God-view and the resulting warped worldview will at best lead to a superficial cure. Your healing will certainly involve the spiritual practice of prayer, as it has for mystics throughout the ages. But it may have to start with questioning authority.

The human race can no longer afford a divisive God-view. The notion of a God separated from us by a gap will inevitably separate us from one another. The great challenge of our time goes beyond religious toleration — beyond putting up with incompatible God-views side-by-side. We need to discover a God-view that unites. Mystics of all religious traditions have glimpsed the same Ultimate Reality that makes each of us whole and all of us one. Wars of religion are clashes not between spiritual people but between religious institutions. The time has come for people within these institutions to affirm and celebrate their unity. The institutions will have to come to terms or die of irrelevance.

It may seem unlikely that we could ever find a God-view that transcends and unites the world's religions. In fact, that God-view has already been found, and you can discover it for yourself by paying attention to your own inner experience of the More that gives your life meaning. We touch upon this "more" whenever we ask the three great questions that make us human.

We ask: "What is really real?" and are confronted with a *silence* more real than anything else; it goes beyond what we can grasp or put into words.

We ask: "Who am I?" and find the More in that depth of our own heart that thoughts cannot fathom nor words express.

We ask: "What is life all about?" and find that our own living and loving is participation in an inexhaustible More of life and love.

Our spiritual and physical well-being depends on our grounding in the experience of these questions — and in the answers that cannot be put into words.

The More into which these questions plunge us pervades our being and yet immeasurably transcends it. Primordial Religion, African or Native American, for instance, confronts each of these three aspects of the More — what I call silence, word, and understanding — as one sacred Presence. Each is still equally emphasized and interwoven with one another as myth, ritual, and right living. But the great traditions that grow out of this primordial matrix — Buddhism, the Western traditions (Christianity, Islam, and Judaism) and Hinduism — pay special attention to one aspect. Emphasis falls more strongly on only one aspect of the More in each of these traditions, whether it be silence, word, or understanding.

Buddhism explores more thoroughly than any other spiritual tradition the abyss of *silence* in which we experience the More as the ground and source of all reality. In his great wordless sermon, the Lord Buddha simply holds up a flower. All those who wait for words are disappointed; the one who understands shows that he does so not by words but by a silent smile. The Buddha, we are told, smiles back and so passes on the core of Buddhist tradition to this, his successor, through silence.

How different are the Western traditions of Judaism, Christianity, and Islam with their emphasis on *word*. Take away the words, and what is left, they ask. Many students of Buddhism in the West seek refuge in silence from what they characterize as "words, words, words." Yet, as T. S. Eliot knew, "words after speech lead into silence." The word, too, can become transparent to the More. All things, people, and situations can be understood as words in which silence speaks. The More comes to word in the "Amen Traditions" — so-called because they share the word "Amen" ("so be it"), the human expression of faith in response to the faithfulness of Ultimate Reality.

The experience of word, listening, and response opens up the possibility of a personal relationship to the More — to the notion of God as personal (though we must not slide into the misunderstanding that God is "a person" like you and me). We come to understand ourselves as divine word, both spoken and addressed. By our response, we become the word we are meant to be. The self-understanding of Jesus as one with "the Father" is a new level of human self-understanding and must not be limited to Jesus. Christian mystics knew this, and Thomas Merton stated it succinctly, "God isn't someone else!"

Swami Venkatesananda offers us a way to understand how Hinduism fits into this scheme when he says, "Yoga is understanding." The English word "yoke" comes from the same root as "yoga," which yokes together word and silence through *understanding*. Understanding comes only when we deeply listen to a word and act on it in such a way that it leads us back into the silence from which it comes. This is also the pivotal point of the Bhagavad Gita: Arjuna's conundrum cannot be solved in any other way than by acting. There is an aspect of the More that we cannot come to know except through doing. It is this aspect on which Hinduism focuses through yoga in all its forms.

In a wholesome spiritual life we find access to the one inexhaustible More along these three pathways: silence, word, and understanding. Early Christian tradition expressed this mystical insight by affirming that "Father," "Son," and "Holy Spirit" are the one God. This implied a pan-*en*-theistic God-view — distinguished from Pantheism (all is God) by the little syllable "en" (= "in"). God is *in* all and all is *in* God (the More that is always more than all). But the notion of God as the absolutely Other was so deeply engraved in the Western mind (and so advantageous for authoritarian institutions) that this wild and wonderful God-view had to be domesticated. Christian theologians objectified mystical insight of God as triune, and projected it onto the God-Out-There. The time was not yet right.

Today, however, all of us can reclaim the Trinitarian (panentheistic) God-view. It is not a Christian monopoly but rather a model familiar to mystics in every tradition. This God-view gives full scope to each of the traditions in its own right, encourages each of them to learn from others who focus on a different aspect of the inexhaustible divine More, and makes them realize that "exploration into God" is a task to which we must all rise together.

Silence, Word, and Action: A Mystic's Guide to Prayer

Prayer in the widest sense happens whenever we open up to that infinite "More" that gives meaning to the finite reality in which we live. In peak experiences, we perceive this More in a flash, but we can prepare ourselves through spiritual practice to receive it as a steady light.

Silencing our mental noise prepares us for an encounter with the More. Or, we can learn to listen so deeply to what our senses perceive that the More — which goes beyond sensuous reality — speaks to us through sight, sound, touch, smell, and taste. Any activity, if we can learn to become fully one with it, can also open us up to its More — in an understanding that comes only by doing.

1. Silence is hard to come by. Most of us live under a constant bombardment of noise — so much so that we

take for granted traffic noise, *Muzak,* and constant chatter. Have you left your TV on, unaware that no one is listening? Take this as a warning signal that noise pollution is endangering your health. "All that lasts long is quiet," says the poet Rainer Maria Rilke. We wouldn't last long unless our bodies insisted on quieting us down in sleep. For our inner health, too, we need periods of being still. Stillness heals. A broken arm needs a cast to keep it still, or else it will not heal. To quiet our inner restlessness, we need a spiritual practice that has silence for its goal. Spiritual silence is more than mere absence of inner noise. It is the More that we experience when we go beyond the reach of words and thought. Many different practices belong to this world of prayer, called Prayer of Silence. All of them aim at leaving the world of the senses behind in order to dive into a fathomless More, an ocean of wordless meaning. Don't let this scare you. Just making room in your schedule for a few minutes of deliberate silence will be a good beginning. You will soon witness how much this does for your inner and outer well-being.

2. Another whole world of prayer consists of spiritual practices that go in the opposite direction from Prayer of Silence and yet, paradoxically, lead to the same goal. There, we left the world of the senses behind; here, it becomes the gate through which we enter the More. This, too, needs spiritual practice, since normally we live merely at the surface. But when we turn our deep attention, heart attention, to the smallest part of reality, it speaks to us, as it were. We receive it as not just say, a dandelion or a sparrow or as some object made by human hands, but as the More speaking to us in dandelion language — unique and untranslatable. Thus we find meaning, which is essential

for human well-being. We cannot survive without it. And "meaning" in this sense is not the significance of a word that you can look up in a dictionary. What is truly meaningful to you? It is some encounter or activity in which your heart finds rest — for a while, at least. "Restless is our heart" until it finds rest in the More, as Augustine pointed out. We can tap this source by turning to the More through any of innumerable things around us and being nourished by meaning. That makes the second world of prayer possible. This is why all the different practices of this second world of prayer are called "living by the Word."

3. All teachers know that understanding comes through doing. By doing whatever we do with total attention — like the concentration of a dervish's whirl — we discover quickly that there is more involved than our own effort, and More in the full sense. The very vitality of our bodies is a mystery to us; it "has us" as much as we "have it." So too, with inner reality. When we are "in" love, we are immersed in More. We somehow understand love only by loving, vitality only by being alive and active. Another name for this participation in the More is "blessing." The English word comes from the same root as "blood." In peak moments we are blessed and can bless. At other times, also, we can deliberately let the bloodstream of blessing flow through us, consciously breathe the life-breath of the universe. The technical term for practices that foster understanding of the More through full attention to what we're doing — from sacred rituals to doing the dishes — is "Contemplation in Action."

Prayer as Silence, Word, and Action is the very core of spirituality, the very essence of health. It calms, nourishes, and enlivens body and soul through communion with the More.

This Is It!

Remember what we said earlier about our peak moments, our glimpses of meaning, and our spontaneous exclamation, "This is it!" The Christian perspective betrays itself by emphasizing the first word of this little sentence: THIS is it! Enthusiasm for the discovery that "God speaks," that everything is Word of God, makes us exclaim again and again, "THIS is it!" and "THIS is it," whenever we are struck by another Word that reveals meaning. Not so Buddhism. Buddhism in turn is struck by the one Silence that comes to Word in so great a multitude and variety of words. "This is IT," Buddhism exclaims; and this and this and this, every one of all these words, is always IT, is always the one Silence. We need Hinduism to remind us that what really matters is that this IS it — that Word IS Silence and Silence IS Word — therein lies true Understanding. The perspectives complement one another.

By appreciating other perspectives, we learn to broaden our own, without losing it. In fact, our understanding of our own tradition is likely to deepen through contact with others. Christians, for instance, may see the mystery of the triune God reflected in the pattern of Word, Silence, and Understanding. God, whom Jesus calls, "Father" can also be understood as that motherly womb of Silence from which the eternal Word is born, before all time, as by God's Self-Understanding, the Silence comes to Word. The Word, the Son, in turn, obediently carries out the Father's will and in doing so returns to God through that Understanding which is perfect love, the Holy Spirit.

CHAPTER 8

SHADOWS

To have hope, we first need to be realistic, says Brother David. We need to get beyond our own optimism or pessimism and acknowledge the contrasts that are a natural part of human existence. That means taking in the light of our aspirations but also confronting the shadows of those things that do not fit into the neat patterns we've come to expect.

"Shadow" is a psychological term introduced by Swiss psychiatrist Dr. Carl G. Jung. It is everything in us that is unconscious, repressed, undeveloped, and denied. These are dark rejected aspects of our being as well as our light undeveloped potential. We all have a shadow and a confrontation with the shadow, is essential for self-awareness.

An inability to recognize and integrate dark and light aspects surrounds us. It is evident in popular culture's linear concept of happiness and also in Christianity's only fledgling attempts at a more balanced perspective that acknowledges the reality of "divine darkness." It is evident too in our own misunderstandings and confusion — from unrealistic ideals about moral perfection that haunt us to notions of a perfect God who consequently remains "foreign to our human heart."

To help move us toward an "integrated wholeness," Brother David turns to Jesus in this essay. Jesus lived with the tension of shadows and light, and, in the end, he embraced a darkness so real that it resulted in his despair. But this point of total abandonment culminating in his crucifixion, Brother David says, is the true resurrection. It is the moment when hope became possible for him as it can be for each of us. For true hope comes when, in our openness to all of life, we remain "open to the possibility of surprise when everything turns out worse than we could ever imagine."

Is the wallowing in pessimism that is so common today simply the flip side of a culture where everyone is expected to just keep smiling and "have a nice day"? Someone says, "How are you?" and you automatically reply, "Fine." Have you ever said anything else? Perhaps, but this took some daring and, like a missed beat in a drum roll, it likely did not go unnoticed. This is because "How are you?" is not really a question, but a greeting, and "Fine" is not really an answer but an acknowledgment of the greeting. "How are you?" "Fine." The two are inseparable.

After repeatedly asserting "fine," a person tends to stifle any other possibility. But sooner or later, what you suppress begins to lead its own life, creeping up slowly and taking hold of you from behind. The *shadow* of the unacknowledged becomes like a subconscious monster, life-denying and confronting you with all sorts of things that are difficult to deal with, let alone integrate into the core of who you are. The shadow — now not seen together with the light but instead as separated from the light — is prone to perversions, distortions and a variety of unhealthy developments.

This is why a healthy personality does not suppress the dark side, *the shadow,* but accepts it, values it, even embraces it, and so becomes whole.

Neither optimism nor pessimism is desirable because neither is realistic. When we are in an optimistic mood, we are not interested in reality. We might say, "Don't confuse me with facts, I am an optimist." Correspondingly, when we are in a pessimistic mood we are unconcerned with reality. When we are confronted with good news we commonly respond, "That won't last," or we find a flaw, regardless of the degree of truth. The attitude that truly deals with reality is what religious language defines as hope.

Hope is miles apart from both pessimism and optimism. Because hope deals with reality and because surprise is essential to reality, hope is openness to that surprise. In the full religious sense, hope is not necessarily optimism, or the conviction that everything will turn out fine. Despair, not hopelessness, is the opposite of hope, and hope thrives in the midst of hopelessness when it will not give in to despair. When a situation appears hopeless, there is always room for surprise. To have hope is not to seek the surprise of a Hollywood happy ending, which is unrealistic optimism. To have hope is to remain open to the possibility of surprise when everything turns out worse than we could ever imagine. Despair assigns reality a deadline, whereas hope knows that there are no deadlines. This is how hope truly thrives in the midst of hopelessness.

Today we often cheapen hope to optimism, and so when things don't work out picture perfect, we get the backlash of wallowing in pessimism and despair. Despair blocks surprises from reality; hope paves the way for reality to surprise itself.

If we have hope, we create a hopeful reality. Our openness for surprise challenges reality. It is like a mother who sees in her child the possibility and potential of new life. By maintaining this hope the mother is saying to the child, "surprise me," and as a self-fulfilling prophecy, the child surprises her. The child surprises himself as well in the process. We surprise ourselves if we live up to the expectations of somebody who looks at us with eyes of hope and thereby creates the space into which we can grow. This motherly attitude is the one we ought to have toward people who are caught up in pessimism or despair, rather than to write them off or contradict them. That would be what they want: to be contradicted. But rather look at them with eyes that say "surprise me," and they will.

In contrast to some other traditions, the Christian tradition has not done particularly well in cultivating a practical method for integrating *the shadow*. In its enthusiasm for the divine light, Christian theology has not done justice to the divine darkness. This is part of the reason we have some of the problems that plague us, especially in our efforts to be moral. If you are striving to be perfect and pure, everything depends on getting the right idea of what absolute purity and perfection mean. We tend to get trapped in the idea of a static perfection that leads to rigid perfectionism — and an image of God that is foreign to the human heart. Religious doctrine has created an image of God that is totally purged of anything that we call dark. Therefore when we try to live up to the standards of a God that is purely light we cannot handle the darkness within us and we suppress it. But the more we suppress it, the more it takes hold of us because it is not integrated or even acknowledged. Before we know it we are in serious trouble.

You can get out of that trap if you come back to the core of the Christian tradition, to the real message of Jesus. You find him, for instance, saying, "Be perfect as your heavenly Father is perfect." Yet he makes it clear that this is not the perfection of suppressing the darkness, but the perfection of integrated wholeness. That's the way Matthew puts it in the Sermon on the Mount. Jesus talks of our Father in heaven who lets the sun shine on the good and the bad, and lets the rain fall on the just and the unjust alike. It's both the rain and the sun, not only the sun. And it's both the just and the unjust. Jesus stresses the fact that God obviously allows the interplay of shadow and light. God approves of it. If God's perfection allows for tensions to work themselves out, who are we to insist on a perfection in which all tensions are suppressed?

In his own life, Jesus lived with tension and embraced darkness. And as Christians we see in Jesus what God is like. That's really what Christians believe about Jesus: in this man who is fully human — like us in all things except our alienation, our sinfulness — in this human we can see what God is like. And this human being died, crying out, "My God, why have you forsaken me?" At that moment darkness covers the whole earth, which is, of course, a poetic statement, not necessarily a historic account of what happened then. At that moment God reaches the greatest distance from God's own being and embraces the darkness of utmost alienation. If God's reality can embrace the one who cries out, "My God, why have you forsaken me?" and is, for all practical purposes, forsaken of God, and dies, then everything is embraced — death and life and every tension between them. And that moment is, according to the Gospel of John, not the prelude to the resurrection, not something that is then reversed by the resurrection, but is the resurrection. Jesus says earlier, "When I am lifted up from the earth, I shall draw all things to myself." According to the theology of the Gospel of John, the lifting up is the lifting up on the cross. His death on the cross is the moment of his glory; it's an upside-down glory. It's the ultimate shame for someone to be executed on the cross. But for the eyes of faith Jesus is "lifted up." That is the resurrection. That is the ascension. That is also the pouring out of the spirit: he dies with a loud cry — that means with power, not with a whimper — and he hands over his spirit. At that moment the whole world is filled with the divine spirit. The vessel is broken and the fragrance fills the whole house. It's all profoundly poetic. You cannot understand the Gospel of John without a sense of poetry. It is a poem from beginning to end. Because we have often failed to read it in that way, we get into all sorts of traps.

The moral implications of all this are deeply anchored in the Christian tradition from its earliest statements on. We touch here the rock-bottom of the Christian tradition. Yet this integration of light and darkness hasn't been explored properly. This is the problem. Traditions do not always develop evenly. We have only had two thousand years. There are much older traditions. Give us another two thousand years and we may catch up.

Right now we are at an important stage of transition. We are beginning to look at certain areas that we haven't faced for a very long time. This area of integrating the shadow is one of them. Martin Luther saw it and the Reformation was a period in which this area was bravely faced. (It's too bad that there were so many diplomatic mistakes made on both sides, that the whole thing didn't lead to a renewal of the Church, but rather to a split of the Church.) Luther stressed a key conviction of the New Testament, which the Catholic Church is only now recognizing, that is, "by grace you have been saved." That's one of the earliest insights in the Christian tradition: it's not by what you do that you earn God's love. Not because you are so bright and light and have purged out all the darkness does God accept you, but as you are. Not by doing something, not by your works, but gratis you have been saved. That means you belong. God has taken you in. God embraces you as you are — shadow and light, everything. God embraces it, by grace. And it has already happened.

But where does the moral struggle come in? We all know it has to come in somewhere. St Paul, who says, "By grace you have been saved," encourages us in the next chapter, "Now live worthy of so great a gift." That's a totally different thing, however, from trying to earn it. Many Christians struggle to earn the great gift. How can you earn a gift? I'm simply telling you what Jesus taught, what Paul taught, what the Christian tradition at its core teaches.

Paul says, "Be angry, but do not sin." That has a contemporary ring for us. Sin is alienation. Do not let your anger separate you from others, but don't suppress your anger either. Be angry, all right. But "do not let the sun set over your anger." That is again a poetic statement. It may mean, literally, before evening, make up. That's one of the clearest meanings of it. But it may also mean never, not even at this moment when you are angry, let the sun set over this shadow. You see how beautifully it's expressed. Do not let the sun go down over your anger. Do not let your anger lead to alienation.

I can only touch upon these things, but I hope that it at least gives you a taste and makes you realize that when you go deeply into the Christian tradition, whether it is your own or not, you will find all these things. They are there. But then you ask, "Why don't we ever hear of it? Why hasn't it been developed?" Well, it hasn't been sufficiently developed yet. But you are there. You have your share to contribute. When you are through with your tradition, it must be different from what you found or else you have failed. It is your responsibility to make your religious tradition, whatever it may be, Christian or otherwise, more truly religious by the time you are through with it. That's the great challenge we face.

PART THREE

Living Our Spirituality

Can we make the transition and live what we know is true and good? Can we become fully alive in our mind, body, and spirit and live as if we really do belong together? If we take this leap and commit to making our spirituality our own, then what can we expect and what will be expected of us?

This final group of essays provides a glimpse into this next step as seen through Brother David's eyes. He writes about both the path he has chosen as a monk and the path, he says, we all travel when we decide to "live from the heart." Mystic and humanist, he talks about the price to be paid if we want to develop mindfulness, become whole, and live in peace. More interior work and searching are still required. But we can also begin to act on our convictions, and Brother David provides steps to start us on our way. His willingness to travel his path becomes our invitation to find our way. The inspiration of these essays is found in his daily taking to heart what he knows to be true.

CHAPTER 9

LEARNING TO DIE

One of the challenges that Brother David helps us to face in this essay is to take an honest look at our views about death and what we think will occur after we die. He finds this critical for Westerners, especially those belonging to a religion. The high value we place on our individuality and our independence is at work even in the realm of death. This can dull the impact of death's finality, and just as important, it can dull our ability to embrace the gift of this life.

The real lessons in how to die are found in living, Brother David reminds us. We die, in fact, a bit every day. Growing requires us to die to what we are in order to become what we are not. A prerequisite for loving relationships is a continual letting go. This "inner gesture" of giving ourselves is never easy. Risks are involved because we are turning over responsibility without knowing the outcome. But we know this much: Not to take the risk is the real death — the exclusion of ourselves from the "free flow of life." In the end, we have only what we give up, he tells us. "What we hold on to deteriorates in our grasp."

The only point where one can start to talk about anything, including death, is where one finds oneself. And for me this is as a Benedictine monk. In the rule of St. Benedict, the *memento mori* — the remembrance of death — has always been important. One of what St. Benedict calls "the tools of good works" is to have death at all times before one's eyes. When I first came across the Benedictine Rule and tradition, this was one of the key sentences that impressed and attracted me very much. It challenged me to incorporate the awareness of death into my daily living, for that is what it really is saying. This doesn't mean thinking of one's last hour, or of death as a physical phenomenon. It is seeing every moment of life against the horizon of death, with the challenge to incorporate that awareness of dying into every moment and thus to become more fully alive.

I have found that this approach is present — sometimes more explicitly, sometimes more implicitly — in all the different spiritual traditions that I have encountered. It is certainly very strong in Zen Buddhism; it is present in Hinduism and Sufism. It is one of those basic human responses by which a person confronts meaning in order to live religiously. I use the term "religiously" here to refer to the quest for ultimate meaning. Death is evidently one of the most important elements in this quest for it puts the whole meaning of life into question. We may be preoccupied with purposeful activities, with getting tasks accomplished, our work completed, but then circumstances change and we find ourselves facing our final death or one of those many deaths that we go through day by day. Suddenly, purpose is not enough; we seek meaning in our lives. When we come close to death and we can no longer manipulate and control things to achieve specific goals, we focus on whether our life can still be meaningful.

This question may help us to understand why in the monastery we are counseled (or challenged) to have death at all times before our eyes. Monastic life is one way of radically confronting the question of life's meaning. You cannot get stuck *in purpose* in the monastery: there are many purposes connected with it, but they are all secondary. This is because as a monk, you are not closely tied into the grid of societal obligations. Your role in the world is, in a real sense, totally superfluous, and so you cannot evade the question of meaning.

As we have seen in chapter 2 ("The Monk in Us") the distinction that I am making between purpose and meaning isn't always carefully maintained in our everyday language and thought. In fact, we could avoid a good deal of confusion in our lives if we did pay attention to the distinction. It takes only a minimum of awareness to realize that our inner attitude when striving to achieve a purpose, a concrete task, is clearly different from the attitude we assume when something strikes us as specially meaningful. With purposeful activities, we must be active and in control. With a meaningful experience, it is a matter of savoring the world around us. The idioms we use when referring to meaning tend to be more passive than active. But remember, we do not want to play off purpose against meaning, or activity against passivity. It is merely a matter of trying to adjust the balance in our hyperactive, purpose-ridden society. We distinguish between purpose and meaning not in order to separate the two, but in order to unite them. Our goal is to let meaning flow into our purposeful activities by fusing activity and passivity into genuine responsiveness.

Death puts our responsiveness to the ultimate test. Unless our dying becomes our full and final response to life, activity and passivity must ultimately clash in death. Because we are so one-sidedly active in life, we think of death one-sidedly as passive. In death we are indeed passive: obviously, dying is the most passive thing that can happen to us. It is the ultimate passivity — something that will happen to us inevitably. We will all be killed in one way or another, whether it be by disease or by old age or by an accident or in some other way. We are well aware of this aspect but not too many people realize that death is also ultimate activity. Some "symptomatic idioms" can help make this clear. It is, for example, very significant that the one act that is the most passive in our experience, namely dying, cannot be expressed in English by a passive form. There is no passive voice to the verb to die. We can be killed, but we have to die. There is imbedded into our very language the realization that dying is not only passive, maybe not even primarily passive, but also the ultimate activity. Dying is something we have to do. These two things have to come together in death: we do something and we suffer something. More than that: we must suffer what we do and do what we suffer.

This doing and suffering, this give and take, which constitutes responsiveness, is brought into focus by our confrontation with death, but it has a far wider range. It characterizes life in all its aspects. Life, if it isn't a give and take, is not life at all. The taking corresponds to the active phase, to our "purpose" when we do something; while the giving of ourselves to whatever it is that we experience is the gesture by which meaning flows into our lives. It must be stressed over and over that this is not an either/or; life is not a give or take, but a give and take; if we only take or only give, we are not alive. If we only take breath in we suffocate, and if we only breathe out we also suffocate. The heart pumps the blood in and pumps it out; and it is in the rhythm of give and take that we live. In practice, however, the balance is often upset in our lives. Our emphasis falls far too heavily on the taking, on the doing, on the purpose. We belong to an "underdeveloped nation" with regard to meaningful living. Because we keep cultivating only one-half of the give and take of life, we are only half alive.

Here again the idioms we use are symptomatic of our preoccupation with taking and with purpose. We have scores of idioms that speak of taking but few that speak of giving yourself; we take a walk, take an exam, take a trip, take a course, take a bath, take a rest, take a meal. We take practically everything, including many things that nobody can truly take, such as time. We say we take time; but we really live only if we give time to what takes time. If you take a seat, it is not a very comfortable way of sitting down, but if you let the seat take you that's more like it. Taking a nap is the surest way to insomnia, for as long as you insist on taking it you will never get it; but the moment you give yourself to it you will fall asleep.

We might begin to suspect that our one-sided insistence on taking not only prevents us from living balanced lives and living peacefully, but also from dying a balanced death and dying peacefully. After a life in which we take and take, we eventually come up against something which we can't take; death takes us. This is serious. One can go through life taking, and in the end all this will add up to having taken one's life, which is, in a real sense, suicide.

But we can learn to give ourselves. It doesn't come easy, conditioned as we are to be fearful of giving ourselves, but it can be learned. In learning to give ourselves we learn both to live and to die — to die not only our final death, but those many deaths of daily living by which we become more alive.

This is precisely the point: whenever we give ourselves to whatever presents itself, instead of grasping and holding on, we flow with it. We do not arrest the flow of reality, we do not try to possess, we do not try to hold back, but we let go. Everything is alive as long as we let it go. When we cut the flower it is no longer alive; when we take water out of the river it is just a bucketful of water, not the flowing river; when we take air and put it in a balloon it is no longer the wind. Everything that flows and is alive has to be taken and given at the same time — taken with a very, very light touch. Here again we are not playing off give against take, but learning to balance the two in a genuine response to living as well as to dying. I remember a story told me by a young woman whose mother was close to death. She once asked her: "Mother, are you afraid of dying?" and her mother answered, "I am not afraid, but I don't know how to do it." The daughter, startled by that reply, lay down on the couch and wondered how she herself would do it if she had to; and she came back with the answer: "Mother, I think you have to give yourself to it." Her mother didn't say anything then but later she said. "Fix me a cup of tea and make it just the way I like it, with lots of cream and sugar, because it will be my last cup of tea. I know now how to die."

This inner gesture of giving yourself to "it," of letting go from moment to moment, is what is so difficult for us, but it can be applied to almost any area of experience. The giving up is a real death, a real dying; it costs us an enormous amount of energy, the price, as it were, that life exacts from us over and over again for being truly alive. For this seems to be one of the basic laws of life; we have only what we give up. We all have had the experience of a friend admiring something we owned, when for a moment we had an impulse to give that thing away. If we follow this impulse — and something may be at stake that we really like, and it pains for a moment — then for ever and ever we will have this thing; it is really ours; in our memory it is something we have and can never lose.

It is all the more so with personal relationships. If we are truly friends with someone, we have to give up that friend all the time. We have to give freedom to that friend — like a mother who gives up her child continually. If the mother hangs on to the child, first of all, it will never be born; it will die in the womb. But even after it is born physically it has to be set free and let go over and over again. So many difficulties that we have with our mothers, and that mothers have with their children, spring exactly from this, that they can't let go; it is much more difficult for a mother to give birth to a teenager than to a baby. But this giving up is not restricted to mothers; we must all mother each other, whether we are men or women. I think mothering is just like dying, in this respect; it is something that we must do all through life. And whenever we do give up a person or a thing or a position, when we truly give it up, we die — yes, but we die into greater aliveness. We die into a real oneness with life. Not to die, not to give up, means to exclude ourselves from that free flow of life.

Giving up is very different from letting go or letting someone down; in fact, they are exact opposites. Giving up is an upward gesture, not a downward one. Giving up the child, the mother upholds and supports him, as friends must support one another. We cannot let down responsibilities that are given to us, but we must be ready to give them up, and this is the risk of living, the risk of the give and take. Sometimes, we may be tempted to substitute letting go but that sounds too passive. Giving up is the truly sacrificial gesture. There is a tremendous risk involved, because when you really give up, you don't know what is going to happen to the thing or to the child. If you knew, the sting would be taken out of it, but it wouldn't be real giving up. When you hand over responsibility, you have to trust. That trust in life is central to all the religious traditions. It is called by different names; Christians know it as faith, and in Zen Buddhism, to my surprise, it is also called faith, though with a connotation different from the one it has in the biblical tradition. It isn't faith in anything or anyone, but there is a lot of emphasis in Buddhist monasteries on the tension between faith and doubt, faith always being a nose's length ahead of doubt. The greater your doubt, the greater your faith will be — faith in ultimate reality, faith in yourself, if you wish, your true Self. But in the Buddhist as well as in the Christian tradition faith is courage — the courage to take upon yourself the risk of living, and dying, because the two are inseparable.

Thus, one could distinguish between two ways of dying: a mere giving in, which means you are being killed without really dying; and a vital way of dying, a giving up, which is this giving of yourself and so dying into deeper life. But that takes a great deal of courage, because it is always a risk, a step into something unknown. It also takes a great deal of vitality, and that is why I am a little reluctant to accept what Karl Rahner and Ladislas Boros have to say about death. They are two German Catholic theologians who have written with a great deal of insight on death, but both put much weight on their ideas of what happens in a person's last moments. I would much rather say: die when you are alive, because you don't know how well you will be able to do something that takes all your energy when you are senile, weak, or very sick.

Here again is one of the points where I think birth and death come very close to one another: neither of the two events can be precisely pinned down to a moment in time. We don't really know when a person is born. We can point to the physical fact of the umbilical cord being cut, but some people come to life maybe after forty years, or even later. When does a person come to life? I can imagine that the very moment in which someone comes to life is also the moment in which he really dies. And everything that led up to that, for forty-five years perhaps, is time spent in practicing for the important moment; and everything that follows is time spent letting nature run its course. Maybe in some people's lives this happens all of a sudden, at one moment, while with others it is a gradual thing that goes laboriously through many stages.

Most of what I have said simply means: let's learn to die so that, when our last hour comes and if we are still alert to it, we will be able to die well. But at any rate let's learn it, and that means let's learn to give ourselves over and over again to that which takes us; let's give up as a mother gives up. In many traditions you have this notion that throughout our lives we train for a right dying; and that means to train for flowing with life, for giving ourselves. And this suggests some more symptomatic idioms of taking and giving that show ways we can make the inner gesture of dying: giving thanks instead of taking for granted; giving up rather than taking possession; forgiving as opposed to taking offense. What we take for granted does not make us happy; what we hold on to deteriorates in our grasp; what we take offense at we make into a hurdle we can't get past. But in giving thanks, giving up, forgiving, we die here and now and become more fully alive.

We speak, for instance, of a good death versus a bad death: I suppose the death we call bad is the one in which we struggle and cannot die peacefully. There are many cases when the doctor says: "I don't know how this patient keeps on living," but perhaps he never learned to let go, so he hangs on for dear life, as we say. He will eventually be killed, but he has not learned to give himself freely. After all, it is not a dogma or a theory but something that anyone can check out and experience in his own life, that when we really give up and actively die, we die not into death but into a richer life; and when we drag on and hang on to something that we should have already let go of, we are dead and decaying. Thus we know — not from any revelation but from our own personal daily experience — that the fruit of a good death, a death to which we give ourselves, is greater fullness of life, and the fruit of a death against the grain, in which we are just killed and do not give ourselves, is destruction, or what the Bible calls the second death.

Now the difficulty that comes in here is that when it is a matter of our final physical death, what is given up by us is all of life. I feel rather strongly that we sometimes fail — especially, I think, people who speak from a religious perspective — to stress the seriousness of dying. It may be a beautiful image, but it just won't do to say that "we fall asleep." Death is not falling asleep; nor is it the same as going into a tunnel and coming out on the other side. I also am not concerned with and do not like to speak of "afterlife." When speaking about the event through which all we know of life comes to an end, in every respect, it makes no sense to talk about life after death because death is the end of time for the one who dies. And that is just what I mean. Death is the event which has no after. To blur this fact means losing sight of the seriousness of dying.

It is an all too harmless picture of death if we think that the body dies but the soul lives. Is there really an independent soul over against a body with its own independent existence? Concretely we experience ourselves as body-soul beings. The total person, experienced from the outside, is body. Experienced from the inside, that same total person is soul. In that event we call death, the total person comes to an end. But the total person that sits here now and talks knows that whenever in his life anything truly died, it did not mean destruction, but always a step into greater life; and therefore, that total person can take the leap of faith and can say yes, I believe that in this ultimate death also, what I am going toward is ultimate life. And that is faith in the resurrection, in the Christian context, because resurrection is not survival; it is not revivification, or coming back to life or any sort of reversal at all. The flow of life cannot ever be reversed. By faith we die forward into fullness of life.

This is why eminent Christian theologians today can dispense with the notion of an immortal soul without jeopardizing the Good News of resurrection and eternal life. In fact, as soon as we no longer feel obliged to hold on to such intellectual abstractions as the notion of an immortal soul, we are able to enter more freely and more fully into the existential approach on which biblical statements about the resurrection are based. We might be surprised to discover that even the Christian belief in the resurrection of the body is simply based on the experience that soul and body are existentially one in the human person. It is not possible to speak of a disembodied human being, because that is no longer a human being. The body absolutely belongs to it. Therefore, when St. Paul speaks of resurrection life — life beyond death as I would call it, rather than after death (if death is the end of time, then what's after it?) — he speaks about life that must be embodied.

What happens in the course of our lives is that we become somebody. Who we become will depend on the decisions we make and somehow *bodily enact*. It will depend on the responses we give to God's calling, which reaches us in many different forms, and these responses, too, will be *bodily enacted*. That we become somebody in this way is obviously as much a statement about our bodies as it is a statement about our souls. But the body we call our own in this sense is not limited by our skins. It comprises all those elements of the cosmos by which we have expressed our own personal uniqueness; it is the total person, seen from the outside. But if the total person has died, resurrection of life, as St. Paul sees it, must be a new creation of the total person — soul and body — by God who alone provides the continuity between the old and the new life. All St. Paul can say about our immortal life, the Christ-life within us, is that it is "hidden with Christ in God" (Col. 3:3). This holds true whether we have died or not. In either case, "your real life is Christ," as St. Paul puts it in the same passage.

Passages like these make it clear that the Christian vision of immortal life is far closer to what has been branded as "Eastern" notions than it is to those popular Western beliefs tied to an immortality of the soul. When Christians practicing under some guru from the East learn to realize "I am not my body, I am not my mind," they are making room for an understanding of St. Paul's words: "Your real life is Christ." All too often this understanding is blocked by the misconception "I am not my body, but I am my mind," a misconception perpetuated by the doctrine of the immortal soul.

It sometimes appears as a threat to Christians that Eastern thought seems to challenge the Western emphasis on individual survival. But is that popular emphasis really in tune with the Christian message? The one thing that is certainly true about it is that personhood, what we have made of ourselves in becoming somebody, is something that will never be lost; but that is a different thing from individuality. We are born as individuals and we become persons, laboriously so. We become persons through relationships with others — interrelationship is what defines you as a person. What separates us defines us as individuals, but what relates us to others makes us persons. It is in the relationship of a deep love that we become most truly persons. When we give and lose ourselves, we paradoxically find our true self. What St. Paul calls our real life, the Christ-self within us, is universal interrelatedness in love; and it is not difficult to see that this is more readily compatible with "Buddha nature" or "Atman" than with insistence on perpetuating individual separateness.

But now St. Paul says of that Christ-self, which is our real immortal life, not only that it is hidden with Christ in God, but that "when Christ appears, then you too will appear with him and share his glory." This seems so central to the Christian message that I for one feel that I cannot be agnostic about it. I cannot say: "Well, just give me the rest of Christian life and teaching and forget about eschatology." To do something right we must start out with the end clearly in mind. If not even a meal will turn out right if we start with the ingredients instead of a clearly planned menu, we had better keep our eyes on the end of our spiritual life. We ought to clarify our eschatology, traditionally defined as "last things, of the world or of human beings." Our problem at the moment seems to be that we have outgrown our childlike integrity in dealing with eschatological myths, but have not yet achieved the integrity of mature minds capable of accepting these myths more fully than the child could. We are like awkward adolescents who laugh at fairy tales that were deeply meaningful to them not long ago and will be more meaningful still a short time hence.

We might do well to take a fresh look at what we might call the Christian mythology of heaven, hell, purgatory, judgment, and so on. It is more important than we might guess. We cannot assume that it is just something we have outgrown; we have only seen that certain images must not and cannot be taken literally any longer. On the other hand, a Christian can still fully believe in the reality these images try to depict. I can say that I believe in the resurrection of the body and in the last judgment; but I wouldn't press the imagery. I believe in the reality that stands behind these truths but I take the expression very lightly. They are meant to be images, beautiful poetic images, but no more. Actually the myth of purgatory comes very close to the myth of reincarnation; it tries in general to answer the same questions and it comes up with largely the same answers — that there is justice and that you have to work out your karma. But just as I would not press the image of purgatory as if there were actually a fire burning somewhere with so many degrees of heat, so I personally would not press the imagery of reincarnation. But I can say that I do believe in both.

One reason why Christian tradition has always steered me away from preoccupation with reincarnation has not so much to do with doctrine as with spiritual practice. The finality of death is meant to challenge us to decision, the decision to be fully present here now, and so begin eternal life. For eternity rightly understood is not the perpetuation of time, on and on, but rather the overcoming of time by the now that does not pass away. But we are always looking for opportunities to postpone the decision. So if you say: "Oh, after this I will have another life and another life," you might never live, but instead keep dragging along half dead because you never face death. Don Juan says to Carlos Castaneda, "That is why you are so moody and not fully alive, because you forget you are to die; you live as if you were going to live forever." What remembrance of death is meant to do, as I understand it, is to help us make the decision. Don Juan stresses death as the adviser. Death makes us warriors. If you become aware that death is right over your left shoulder and if you turn quickly enough you can see him there, that makes you alive and alert to decisions.

As human beings, here and now, not as believers of this or that doctrine, we all know what life beyond time means. If we can say now, and know what we mean when we say now, we are speaking about a reality that is not in time. The now is; time is only possibility for becoming. Dying in all its forms and stages is our opportunity to pass from time into the now that does not pass away, from the mere possibility of becoming to being real.

In our human experience time is, to use a fine expression I heard somewhere, a measure for the energy it takes to grow. In that sense it has nothing to do with minutes and hours, years and eons, with clock time. And growing means to die to what we are in order to become what we are not yet. The seed has to die to become a plant, and we have to die to being children in order to become adolescents, and so on. But our most important death has to do with dying to our independence, as individuals, and so coming to life as persons in our interdependence. We find this terribly difficult because we always want to retain our independence, the feeling that "I don't owe anybody anything." Then comes the moment of death, whether it is the ultimate death or a moment in the middle of life, and we give up our independence and come to life in interdependence, which is the joy of belonging and of being together. This is what we really most want, but except for such moments we hang on to something that we don't really want and yet are afraid to let go of — our independence and the isolation that necessarily goes with it. The moment we let it go, we die into the joy of interdependence.

The importance of our physical death fades away in comparison with this dying into what St. Paul calls the real life, Christ in us. He says in another passage: "I live, yet not I; Christ lives in me." This is not a private statement about himself; he means that each one of us ought to be able to say that. As believers, you and I can say that as well as St. Paul; and that means that it is the true Self that lives in all of us; I — "yet not I; Christ lives in me." The face we had before we were born, as the Buddhists put it, is the Christ-reality. That doesn't mean, narrowly, Jesus Christ, Jesus of Nazareth; it means the Christ. It is not separated from Jesus of Nazareth but is not limited to him. It comes very close to what Buddhists call Buddha nature, and Hindus call Atman, the lasting reality. But we are still afraid of losing our individuality in this all-embracing unity. I think we could overcome this fear by seeing that Divine Oneness is not achieved by the imposition of uniformity, but by the embracing of limitless variety; there is room for all our personal differences within it.

One time I talked with Eido Shimano Roshi about Zen Buddhists' perspective on the question of the personality or impersonality of this ultimate reality. There seems to be what is generally thought of as an important difference of concepts here between East and West, or between the Buddhists and the Christians. The Buddhists use the image of waves on the sea: each of us is just one wave that comes out and goes back into the sea. I told him that a Westerner does not readily accept this; he or she says,

"I am somebody with self-consciousness, awareness, and self-possession. Am I just going back into some cosmic custard? If that sea out of which I came is impersonal and I am personal, then I would be more than the sea." The answer Eido Roshi gave me was simple enough: "If the sea did not have all the perfection of person-hood, from where would the waves have gotten it?" That is a beautiful Buddhist answer, and it does full justice to the Christian concern. But we could also say: All right, the wave goes back into the ocean, and that is a beautiful picture; but that high point, when the wave was cresting, the moment when it was most alive, that, as T. S. Eliot said, is a moment that was not only in time but "in and out of time." It was one of those now moments that does not pass away, that is eternity. And therefore anything that happens, at that moment of the fullest personhood, simply is; it does not belong to "was" or "will be" but to that which can never again be lost; maybe because it never was unrealized, maybe because it is a bursting forth of the eternal now into time. I experience it as being realized, but perhaps it is my homecoming.

I like the suggestion too that the virgin energy of a life in which personhood was never developed simply returns to the source, a wave that never crested. This image somehow connects with the idea of time running out. But the turning point of the spiritual life is the moment when time running out is turned into time being fulfilled. It rests with us whether death will be a fizzling out when our time runs out or an explosion of the fullness of time into the now of eternity. In the book of Deuteronomy God says: "I place before you today life and death; choose life." Choose life! Life is something we have to choose. One isn't alive simply vegetating; it is by choosing, making a decision, that you become alive. In every spiritual tradition life is not something that you automatically have; it is something that you must choose, and what makes you choose life is the challenge of death — learning to die, not eventually, but here and now.

CHAPTER 10

PATHS OF OBEDIENCE:
FAIRY TALES AND THE
MONK'S WAY

136

Recognizing that "some topics are too heavy to be treated other than lightly," Brother David turns to fairy tales in this essay about the challenges and obstacles faced by those on the "path with a heart." This path is all-embracing and represents a universal quest for love: the timeless tale of romantic love, a monk's search for divine love, or simply, our own falling in love with Love itself.

Snow White and Psyche are the main characters in "Paths of Obedience," and for Brother David both personify "Anima." This is Jung's term for the true inner self that includes intuition, creativity, and imagination, qualities that require our conscious development. Both of these women, in their pursuit of love, have their motives and desires tested with increasing intensity until their integrity and capacity to love are on trial. "Disobedience" pulls each off course, but their actions can be understood only when viewed in the context of love. "Love is our heart's creative 'yes!' to that all-embracing design of being to which we belong — not a static design, of course, but a universal choreography, a dance," says Brother David. "Obedience is the process of finding, step by step, our way into the harmony of that great design, and so into love."

Brother David doesn't offer answers in this essay. Like the authors of fairy tales, he is more concerned about helping us prepare for our own journey on the "path with a heart." For that, he knows, we will have to learn to live with the questions and, like Psyche, learn to live with our invisible Lover.

Some topics are too heavy to be treated other than lightly. Great fairy tales have that light touch. They treat a weighty message with so light a heart that we are forever delighted by the tension between playful form and ponderous content. A fairy tale at its best might well be a myth that has learned its own lesson so well that it is able to take itself lightly.

Like a smile, fairy tales speak a language understood by all and need no translation. This is the reason also why the language of fairy tales seems to me appropriate for speaking about obstacles, tests, and trials on the monastic path. Behind this choice of language stands my conviction that the Path that makes any path worth pursuing is one and the same for all of us. The monk has no monopoly on it. The monastic path is merely a methodical approach, designed to keep one on that great "Path with a heart." Not all who try the monastic approach are thereby monks; what makes a person a monk is that the path works for him or her. The monastic path is not designed for all. But the great Path, which even the monastic approach merely approximates, is all-embracing. Its design shines through every path.

The two fairy tales I explore in this essay let the pattern of the great Path shine through. They tell of tests and trials, of the *dura et aspera,* as St. Benedict calls those "hardships and rough spots" on the way. And they speak in a manner that allows us to see both the universal Path in the particular, and the monastic trials in the light of the great tests we all must undergo, regardless of the way we choose. The first of my two stories is the Grimms' "Snow White." The other one is the tale of Amor and Psyche found in the *Golden Ass,* more correctly called *Metamorphoses* (Book 4:28 to 6:24), by Lucius Apuleius.

But before we try to see what these two stories can show us about obstacles on the path of the monk or any other traveler, a word of caution: let us never press their images, nor, for that matter, my own interpretations. In the spirit of the fairy tale, they want to be held lightly. Almost playfully, their images raise questions rather than provide answers. Who are we to press them into answers? Before they are raised, questions tend to oppress us. But once released, a question can arouse life. The images of myth and, in their own way, great fairy tale images raise questions that are not meant to be answered, but lived.

Try, playfully in this spirit, to look at the setup of the Seven Dwarfs through Snow White's eyes. Does it look domestic or monastic? Seen through the eyes of a monk, it certainly resembles a monastery rather than a household.

To begin with, the place "beyond seven mountains" and far from any other habitation suggests monastic seclusion. And the little ones who live together there do not form a family, but rather a brotherhood of some sort. They share a common table (St. Benedict's much emphasized *mensa communis*) and a common dormitory ("if possible," says St. Benedict, "all are to sleep in one room"). All receive the same: there are seven little settings on the table, each with its own little plate, spoon, knife, fork, and cup; and when they come home each lights his own little lamp. One is reminded of St. Benedict's list of things necessary for the personal use of each monk: "cowl, tunic, stockings, boots, belt, knife, pen, needle, handkerchief, writing tablet." Yet, again in good Benedictine style, the needed things are not issued with military uniformity, but "to each according to need": the shorter the dwarf, the shorter his bed. And with a rather monastic sense of fairness, the one whose bed fits Snow White's size takes turns sharing the beds of the other six, crowding each bedmate for only one hour until the night is out.

This brotherhood of seven — *septenarius sacratus numerus* of the Benedictine Rule — follows a strict schedule of work from morning to nightfall. "Idleness is the enemy of the soul. Therefore, the brethren ought to be occupied at definite times in manual labor." (Walt Disney even adds a monastic detail that the Brothers Grimm have not made explicit: he has them chant as they process in order of seniority.) The order and cleanliness maintained by the Seven Dwarfs strengthens our sense of a monastic atmosphere, for "anyone who treats the monastery property in an untidy or careless way is to be taken to task."

No single trait we have pointed out might be convincing by itself, but taken together they create an image that could hardly be so monastic by mere chance. In fact, the perspective in which the Seven Dwarfs are viewed can easily be recognized as that of peasants living near a monastery. It is an outsider's view, in spite of its familiarity with details, and not unsympathetic. The observer is baffled as much as intrigued. We hear a suppressed chuckle in the voice that mentions precisely those traits that peasants would have found most unfamiliar in a monastery — for example, each one is sleeping in a separate bed. St. Benedict, too, makes a point of this, for it was by no means a general custom. While order and cleanliness are stressed again and again, there is also an element of refinement. There is a tablecloth, and the bed linen is as white as snow. And small as the Seven Dwarfs are, the storyteller is looking up to them and refers to them even as *die Herren,* using the title by which, in my own childhood still, peasants would refer to the monks of a neighboring abbey.

The dwarfs seen in this perspective "digging for gold" also make sense. Given enough time, monasteries tend to acquire wealth. But even apart from this fact, peasants saw gold mainly in church, not so much in their own village church as on a pilgrimage to some monastic shrine. The glass coffin, too, with its golden lettering recalls reliquaries and the monks' calligraphy. Yet the most lively details are remembered not from church, but from the monastic kitchen, where lay people from the neighborhood would be as likely as Snow White to find employment. Both cooking and laundering were done in the kitchen — so was mending and knitting while the stew was simmering. All those are listed as Snow White's duties. But to me the most amusing and convincing little detail is the subtle hint at the monks' insistence (shall we call it a hang-up?) that the meals be on time. St. Benedict seems almost a bit fussy regarding the evening meal. Twice he repeats that "all must be finished while daylight lasts," and every Snow White that ever worked in a monastic kitchen soon learned that when the dwarfs came home at night "the meal had better be ready," as the story puts it — or else.

Surely, the stories of Snow White and of Psyche have a great deal of charm in common. But are there deeper connections between the two? On the very surface level of narrative already we detect remarkable parallels as soon as we look closely. This may surprise us, when we remember that one and a half millennia separate Apuleius from the Brothers Grimm. And yet the similarities make sense as soon as we discover that in both stories the protagonist is the same: Anima. (The Jungian definition fits here, but we shall have to fill in nuances as we go along.)

Anima's obstacle course starts with an obstacle. Neither Snow White nor Psyche is allowed a running start. A first and crucial test stands at the very beginning of both stories. It is, in fact, the impact of collision with this initial obstacle that propels Anima into action. Not a bad beginning for a monastic vocation.

How can one tell that there is promise in a monastic candidate? Two answers given seem diametrically opposed, though each is cogent in its own reasoning. One says that only a candidate who was a success in worldly matters is likely to make a go of it in the monastery, too. The other one argues from the opposition between worldly and monastic values, saying that a candidate fit for the monastery must in worldly circles have been considered a misfit. Paradoxically, a genuine candidate proves both opinions right. Our stories bear out this paradox. Like Snow White, and Psyche as well, Anima is both success and misfit. And she is a misfit precisely because she is a success — because of her surpassing beauty.

By their beauty both Snow White and Psyche are singled out. That same beauty becomes for both of them the first great obstacle, the initial touchstone of their testing. We have called it a surpassing beauty. There is something brand new in that beauty, something the old woman can't match, be she stepmother queen or the jealous mother-goddess Aphrodite. Anima's beauty is surpassing because it is something altogether new. But her being beautiful in an unheard-of way surpasses Anima's own comprehension. And so, her own inner bewilderment becomes the ordeal, which her external trials merely make explicit.

As we follow the succession of events, our two stories run perfectly parallel in their first, "premonastic" phase. The differences in narrative detail make the parallelism of the plots all the more striking. Out of jealousy, the old mother figure seeks to destroy Anima. Snow White is as much in the dark about this as Psyche is. By the time they catch on, their fate is sealed. Both are led into the wilderness and both are destined for death in the prime of life, but are spared by the one whom the old woman commissioned for their undoing. In both cases, he spares them because he looks at their beauty and is moved. One could hardly imagine two more different actors for this part than the old queen's huntsman and Eros himself, but the plot is the same. Out in the wilderness Anima is totally alone — *mutterseehg allem,* it is said of Snow White. Similarly, Psyche, left alone on the summit of a crag, brings to mind Rilke's line, "Exposed on the heart's mountains...." But among the trees of a forest (Dante's "dark woods") both central characters find a meal ready. Still, they remain alone in these welcoming surroundings and in the end both go to bed alone and fall asleep. (What monk does not remember that first night on a monastic cot or mat, that last sigh before a deep sleep?)

This, then, is Anima's flight from worldly ways, her *fuga mundi*. And it is Anima, to be sure, here at the threshold of monastic life. Be it in Bangkok or on Mt. Athos, at Chidambaram or Monte Cassino, the one who seeks admission at the monastery gate is always Anima. St. Benedict uses the feminine "anima" more than half a dozen times in speaking of monks, especially in the context of monastic apprenticeship and training. The novice master is to be *aptus ad hurandas animas* — skilled in winning souls. Souls only? Our word "soul" seems quite inadequate to translate "anima" in this and similar passages. What is meant is certainly not the soul as distinct from the body. "Anima," as St. Benedict uses this term, has far more in common with the biblical *nefesh* than with Plato's psyche: It stands for the whole human person. We might even say that it stands for the root of our wholeness, for our human potential to fall in love with Love as Psyche did. The vocation of Anima is to be a bride.

The tribulations Anima must undergo in the wilderness begin for Snow White almost as soon as she has fled over those seven mountains and valleys and has been received by the brotherhood of the seven little ones. It was a common saying among the Desert Fathers, those forebears of Western monks: "Have you fled into the wilderness? Prepare yourself for battle!" Monastic struggles are not just evitable obstacles on the chosen path. A novice deliberately wants to be tested and tried on this narrow road without bypasses. Tribulations are painful, but welcome.

The *tribulum,* from which the word "tribulation" is derived, is the Roman threshing sledge that separates wheat from chaff. The Rule of St. Benedict offers the image of a fire by which silver is tested. "But in all this," monks rejoice, "we more than overcome through the One who loves us." It is for the sake of the great Lover that Anima finds herself in the wilderness, even though at first, she may be no more clearly aware of this deepest reason than Snow White or Psyche or any other novice.

At first, all is sheer delight: Snow White's humble abode, where every pot and pan has its proper place and sparkles on the shelf, no less than Psyche's magnificent residence with its colonnades and fountains. In every monk's memory, novitiate days have a way of taking on colors of paradise. But a crisis must soon come. "Crisis" is another term that has its roots in a Roman farmer's word for sifting grain. Extremity, panic, perplexity are not essential to crisis; its essence is rather a process of stripping that liberates. "Freedom's just another word for nothing left to lose." This applies also to the kernel stripped of its husk and set free: It applies to the process by which Anima in her novitiate is stripped of worldly ties.

Ties and tying, that is the key image of Snow White's first trial. The queen stepmother, disguised as an old peddler woman, calls out her wares: "Staylaces in all colors!" Yes, they do come in all colors. The family ties that will ensnare Psyche in her troubles are only one kind of ties; it matters little by what kind a novice is entangled. "Come," says the old peddler woman, "let me lace your bodice properly for once." Before she knows it, Anima is all tied up with this or that. And that is the end of her new life. Like one dead, she lies on the ground. Snow White had been warned, but to no avail. Finding her now, the Seven who had been unable to save her by warning her save her by cutting her ties. That's far more painful: violent, almost, but this is the violence of love. Nowhere does this brotherhood show their love more clearly than by cutting the ties at any cost (remember, those were brand new silken laces) and setting Anima free. "Little by little she returned to life," the story says.

But temptation will come again. Three times. In the language of myth that means again and again. If the first temptation was entanglement, the second one is vanity. This means something more serious, of course, than the innocent enjoyment of being good-looking. What makes vanity serious is a morbid preoccupation with self, one's little ephemeral self, for that is lethal.

In our fairy tale, the image for this vanity is an ornament, a comb. The wicked queen barely needed to change her disguise. The forgetfulness of novices is proverbial. And yet mindfulness is what the training of the monk is all about, and that mindfulness does not come easily to Anima. "Go away," says Snow White. "I must not let anyone in." But when she eyes the comb, she is infatuated. And when the peddler woman offers to make her pretty, she thinks no harm. What the story literally says is that "Snow White thought of nothing" — not a flattering but an accurate description of Anima in her novitiate daze. As soon as the poisoned comb touches her hair, the daze becomes a deathlike stupor.

Again it is the *acies fraterna* — as St. Benedict calls the brotherhood that closes ranks when the spiritual struggle gets tough — that comes to Anima's rescue. Again the Seven Dwarfs find Snow White lying on the ground as if dead. But they have not forgotten. Immediately recognizing that it was the stepmother's doing, they find the comb and know they must pull it out. This second failure, however, struck deeper than the first. This time, cutting won't do; the comb has to be extracted. Vanity threatens monastic life closer to the core than external ties.

But, in good fairy tale fashion, Snow White is given a third chance. This time she does remember; but again she fails. This time she does not blunder into her failure; she is outright disobedient. Like Eve, who "saw that the tree was good for food, and that it was pleasant to the eyes, and a tree to be desired," Snow White "lusts after the apple," the story tells us, and she takes and eats. "This time the dwarfs will not be able to bring you back to life again," the queen laughs, and she is right.

The laces had remained on the outside, the comb was merely inserted in her hair, but she swallowed a bit of the apple. Eating is a full engagement. It is communion. Psyche, in the end, will drink the goblet of ambrosia and become immortal. Snow White, here, eats the apple of hatred and dies. Her three trials came closer and closer to the core of her being, closer and closer to the essence of Anima's monastic commitment. The laces first: one is ensnared by ties, but they remain external. Next, the comb: vanity is a morbid turning back on itself of a self that may, however, be in itself still healthy. Disobedience, however, is disintegration, death. But death, in this case, would make no sense if obedience consisted merely in doing what one is told to do. The obedient response to a specific call is merely an exercise, nonetheless an important one. It trains Anima in the skill of being attuned to the call of each moment. Mastery of that skill is accomplished obedience. By being in tune with the whole the heart becomes whole. This wholeness, the goal of every path, is at stake in the testing of obedience.

Through obedience, each thread on the cosmic loom finds its way into the great pattern as it emerges. Through disobedience the threads get entangled. Snow White's silken cords of many colors hint at her entanglement. Psyche, in turn, gets tangled up in family ties. When her invisible lover warns her against her sisters, she begins to miss them all the more keenly, and at length her tears prevail. The wicked sisters are admitted and their envy is aroused by Psyche's bliss. Again her lover warns; Psyche must at least guard his secret from her sisters. But when they come again they get her entangled in the web of her own lies, and on their third visit they pull the snare tight. At last she must admit that she has never seen her lover's face and those two, her kin and yet her foes, persuade her that he is a monstrous serpent. They implore her by the bonds of blood and by the ties of birth that unite them to rid herself of that monster bridegroom.

By now the real issue is clearly in focus: this is a test of faith. Will Psyche trust her divine lover or her all too human kin? "If the joys of your secret love still delight you, and you are content to lie in the embrace of a foul and venomous snake, at least we, your loving sisters, have done our duty."

"Those false she-wolves are weaving some deep plot of sin against you," her lover had warned Psyche. "They will try to persuade you to want to know my face; but I have told you, if you see it once, you will see it no more." Psyche, in reply, had assured him of her faithfulness: "I seek no more to see your face; not even the dark of night can be a hindrance of my joy, for I hold you in my arms, light of my life." And yet "she tossed to and fro" in a crisis of faith; "in the same body she hated the beast and loved the husband."

Like Snow White, Psyche forgot. "She forgot all her husband's warnings and all her own promises." At her sisters' faithless counsel, Psyche lights the lantern and lifts the sharpened razor. But there lies Love himself, fairest of gods! "Even the flame of the lamp, when it beheld him, burned brighter for joy," and "a drop of burning oil fell upon the god's right shoulder." In seven syllables, the collapse of paradise is told: *tacitus avolavit* — he flew away without word.

Anima failed. There is no denying it, not if we take our stand on the storyteller's own ground. One need not deny, of course, that in a sense this failure led to growth for Psyche. Yet it is not the element of disobedience that leads to a happy ending after all, but rather a turning away from it, a change of heart.

Contemplating God's plan in which even sin has its function, Augustine marvels: "Even sin!" — *Etiam peccata!* Paul Claudel paraphrases Augustine with a Basque proverb: "God writes straight, even with crooked lines." We should not rob this insight of its power by making it appear as if failure had been the inevitable, even with originally intended course of events. The paradise toward which we go casts no shadow on the one we lost. What our bliss would have been, we shall never know. Enough for Anima that, even after her fall, "the god her lover left her," not lying on the earth, "but gave her hope."

It is hope that is tested in Psyche's second trial. Our myth, as it stands, leaves us little doubt that Psyche has failed, as the biblical myth leaves little doubt that Adam and Eve have fallen into sin. Yet in both stories there remains a ray of hope. Here, Eros promises to destroy the wicked sisters, "but you," he says to Psyche. "I will only punish thus — by flying from you." This flight of Eros from Psyche is an intriguing variation on Francis Thompson's theme of the Hound of Heaven. In the very flight from her, "this tremendous Lover" pursues Anima, here too, "down the nights and down the days," as day and night she seeks him. The paradox of hope is this: Anima's divine lover pursues her by fleeing from her.

According to the logic of the heart, his pursuit of her must necessarily take the form of flight, or else the hopes she has might be mistaken for the Hope he is.

> All which I took from thee I did but take,
> Not for thy harms,
> But just that thou might'st seek it in My arms.[1]

In its own imagery our story develops the purification of Psyche's hope. As Eros flies away, Psyche follows him with her eyes until, blinded by tears, she can see him no more. In despair she casts herself, then and there, headlong from the brink of a river. Again she has failed. The test of her hope starts out with failure. "But the kindly stream...to do honor to the god who sets even waters ablaze with his fire, quickly caught her up in its current and laid her unharmed upon a bank deep in flowering herbage." It is here that Psyche's long wanderings begin.

Wide open to the road ahead of her, Psyche sets out on her journey of hope. The divine Lover whom she seeks secretly guides her steps and keeps stripping her, one by one, of all her hopes, to make her completely empty, ready to receive him. This stripping takes the form of Psyche's encounter with the Great Mother. Hope is a motherly virtue. Under three different aspects Psyche must meet the mother goddess: as Demeter, Hera, and Aphrodite. I see in this threefold repetition more than the fairy tale's fancy for the number three. Only by putting earth, sky, and sea together can the myth bring out the cosmic fullness of the mother image. Demeter gives fruitfulness to the earth; Hera is queen of the Heavens; Aphrodite was born from the foam of the sea.

But there is also a stepping up in the sequence of the three encounters. Wandering after her lost lover, Psyche sees a temple high on a mountain and says, "How do I know that my lord may not dwell there?" It is a temple of the great Earth Mother, and Demeter appears to Psyche but will not let her stay even for a short rest. She must go on.

In a deep valley, Psyche comes upon another temple, where she begs Hera, goddess of matrimony and of childbirth, for asylum. But again her hope is shattered: she must be on her way. Deep in her heart she knows that she will have to face the divinity under the very aspect that causes all her trouble: Aphrodite, goddess of beauty and love. Wishing "to leave no path of fairer hope untried, however doubtful it might be," she had approached the sacred portals of Demeter and Hera. But she knew that no darkness could hide her safely from "great Aphrodite's inevitable eyes." Now she says to herself: "Your little hopes are shattered. Renounce them boldly!" With this boldness of hope, purged of all hopes, and preparing herself for certain death, Psyche stands at last at Aphrodite's portal.

Here the third phase of her trials begins; now her love is to be tested. And, like her faith and hope, her love is not merely tested by these trials but transformed.

The tests of Psyche's love turn out to be tasks of obedience. This must be so. For obedience is the process by which we find our place in a wholeness to which we belong. Wholehearted assent to that belonging is love. In her obedience to the tasks imposed on her by Aphrodite, Psyche comes to understand and accept her belonging in an ever-wider context. By expanding in this way, her love is transformed from preferential attachment to universal belonging. Love always grows in that way.

> ...Thus, love of a country
> Begins as attachment to our own field of action
> And comes to find that action of little importance
> Though never indifferent.... [2]

Psyche's tasks have cosmic implications, stretching her love throughout earth, water, fire, and air. She cannot fulfill her tasks without the help she receives from fellow creatures that inhabit those four realms. Confronted with corn, barley, millet, poppy seed, chickpeas, lentils, and beans all in one heap, Psyche is dumbfounded by the task of putting like with like, but the ants, "humble nurslings of earth, the mother of all," take pity on their human sister; in no time they separate the whole heap, grain by grain. Next she is commanded to bring some golden wool from rams fierce with fire, but out of the water the voice of a reed tells her when and where she may simply gather the pickings of wool from the thorn bushes. And when Psyche is given the impossible task to fetch water from the top of an inaccessible waterfall, an eagle swoops down, fills the vessel, and carries it back to her through the air. "We know that all things work together for good to them that love God" (Rom. 8:28); and here is "the spouse of Love himself," as the little ants call her in the story.

As Anima's love expands, it deepens; it matures. The stages of love's growing are also depicted in the succession of Psyche's labors of love. Not only does the order of images — seed, summer fields, and barren rock — suggest springtime, harvest, and bleak winter; the heart knows more subtle seasons. It starts with making order. "Friend, for what purpose hast thou come?" St. Benedict solemnly confronts each novice with this question. Sort out your motives! There is only one valid one: "that he truly seek God" — Anima's invisible Lover. Once Psyche has done this sorting out, she has to show how brave she can be. In order to prove that her love is "a most vehement flame" (Cant. 8:6), she has to brave the rams that burn with the sun's fire. But from fortitude in action there is still a long climb to that slippery rock where Psyche stands as if she herself had turned to stone. Sooner or later all paths of love, monastic or otherwise, lead to that point where going on is as impossible as turning back. Anima stands still; but she still stands. At this point "love is most nearly itself."

Now certainly Psyche is no longer a novice. Yet there is one more trial that sums up all the others and somehow was contained in all of them. The ultimate obstacle is death.

Aphrodite adds a fourth task to the conventional triad, which we often find in myth and fairy tale. Psyche has to go and confront the one aspect of the Great Mother she had not yet encountered: Persephone, queen of the nether world, Mother Death. This part of the story is so rich that we cannot even begin to do it justice here, but we ought to focus on one element that is essential in our context: Psyche's final failure. Obedient to Aphrodite's command and to the advice of a "far-seeing tower," she carries out the task of bringing back in a casket beauty, a gift of the eternally young queen of the realm of death. Already she has regained the realm of daylight with her treasure. And what happens now? Disobedient, she opens the box.

Once more we must remember the close bond that unites love and obedience if we want to feel the full impact of our story. Throughout Psyche's last and crucial labor of love her obedience is stressed, but one step from the finish line she falters. Alive, she has descended into the realm of death and obtained that gift of beauty sealed in secret. But as soon as she breaks both seal and command, she falls into a deathlike sleep. By failing in obedience she has failed the test of love. This at least is the verdict of the story. It is our task to understand why this is so.

Love is our heart's creative "yes!" to that all-embracing design of being to which we belong — not a static design, of course, but a universal choreography, a dance. Obedience is the process of finding, step by step, our way into the harmony of that great design, and so into love. But disobedience reverses that progress. Disobedience is dissonance. Suddenly we are out of tune, out of step, out of breath; we have fallen out of love, have cut ourselves off from the flow of the life-giving design. This means death. Disobedient Anima dies. All Psyche's helpers from ant to eagle are powerless now, for she has cut herself off from them. Only the lover can bring Snow White to new life; only Eros can wipe the sleep of death from Psyche's eyes: For love is that "Designer infinite" who can mend every rift, and only Love can work into the grand design even sin — *Etiam peccata!*

We have already seen how closely the stories of Snow White and of Psyche parallel one another throughout their beginning phases, from the initial stumbling block of Anima's surpassing beauty to her welcome in monastic surroundings; we now see how perfectly the two stories mirror one another also in their final phases. Three times Snow White succumbs to temptation — by the colorful laces, the pretty comb, the tasty-looking apple; each time she falls into a deathlike sleep that more and more resembles death. Her entanglement and her vanity lead step by step to her final deadly disobedience. Psyche, too, fails three times, as her faith, her hope, and her love are tested. But in all three of those testings it is her obedience that is tried.

Of course, our text knows no such abstractions as we have used to trace the parallels. Happily, the fairy tale lets truth blossom forth in images. And those images, too, show distinct resemblances. We have noticed before how the motif of Snow White tied up in her silken laces echoes Psyche's entanglement in family ties and deceit. But Snow White's ornamental comb and the forbidden fruit are also reflected in Psyche's final disobedience. Are we not reminded of Snow White's vanity when Psyche plots to steal from the treasure entrusted to her just enough to make herself more attractive? And when she decides to "sip a tiny drop therefrom," she falls into the death-sleep that overcomes Snow White as soon as she tastes a tiny piece of the apple.

Our focus on obedience gives us not only a clue to the pattern underlying both stories; it allows us also to recognize it as the basic pattern of the monastic path. St. Benedict calls it "the road of obedience...so that through the labor of obedience you may find your way back to the One from whom you have strayed loitering in disobedience." When the monk comes up against "impossible tasks," St. Benedict has one simple guideline: "Out of love...in faith...let him obey." "Secure in hope" the monk journeys toward the goal. But this hope is truly open for surprise, not blocked by petty hopes; for "eye has not seen nor ear heard what God has prepared for those who love him" (1 Cor. 2:9). What awaits them is the unheard-of, the unseen lover, Love himself.

Union with the Lover who is also the savior from death is the point toward which the stories of Snow White and of Psyche converge. Even at the darkest moment a ray of promise remains: the sleep merely resembles death. Even the animals that come to mourn Snow White are sitting there more like emblems of hope embroidered on a hanging above the glass coffin. Owl, raven, and dove, the birds of death, burial, and mourning — but the owl came first, we are explicitly told, "and last, a dove." A dove also came last, after Noah had sent out a raven: "and there it was with a fresh olive twig in its beak" (Gen. 8:11). The image is strong.

And then comes that moment when Anima opens her eyes and looks into the eyes of Love bent over her. To be awakened by Love, that is the biblical version among the world's great renditions of the theme of spiritual awakening. Love blinds, we say, but in a deeper sense love is the great eye-opener. "Awake, O sleeper, arise from the dead, and the Anointed One will shine on thee!" (Eph. 5:14). When Snow White opens her eyes, her first words are: "O God, where am I?" And her lover gives the beautiful answer: "You are with me!" Ecce! is the first word of Eros to Psyche, "Look!" and he calls her *misella* — poor little one, *pobrecita*, or as the Hound of Heaven says to Anima at the end of the chase:

> Ah, fondest, blindest, weakest,
> I am He Whom thou seekest![3]

"So let us then rise up at last." St. Benedict calls out to his monks, "for Scripture is arousing us and saying: 'It is high time for us to rise from sleep.' With eyes wide open to the light that makes divine...." Yes, this is an expression of rare daring in Christian literature. Not merely divine light, but light that makes divine — *deificum lumen* — that is what we are to look at. Ecce! St. Benedict, too, calls out to Anima: "Look, in his love the Lord shows us the way of life." No sooner has Eros wiped the death-sleep from Psyche's eyes and put it back into its casket, than he shows her that way of life, the road of obedience: "Make haste to fulfill the task with which my mother has charged you; I will take care of the rest."

The rest is the great wedding feast. But before it can be celebrated Anima must carry the sealed secret of beauty to the goddess of beauty and love. By this act of obedience the story of Psyche comes full circle. It all started with that beauty. From the very start, faith, hope, and love have been at stake in Anima's dealing with that gift —

"surpassing," and that means "not easy to handle." It took courage to bear a beauty, which in its newness surpassed her own comprehension — the courage of faith. The newness of that beauty demanded from her a limitless openness for surprise — the openness of hope. And being the beauty she was demanded a "yes" of love in which, accepting herself, she would surpass herself. The fear, the despair, and the "no" of disobedience paralyzed her beauty into that of a death mask. But she is given a chance to complete the "ultimate task," and "with all speed" she runs. In obedience she surpasses herself in faith, hope, and love. This is Anima's ultimate transformation. The original stumbling block has become the final stepping stone. The goblet of immortality is filled for her and the wedding feast with Love can begin.

It is all pure gift. Her original beauty was gift. Her final glory is gift. And all the suffering along the way turns out to have been a gift, so as to make it clear that her overcoming, while truly her own, is also truly gift.

But was it necessary, all that suffering, we ask?

Ah! Must —
Designer infinite! —
Ah! Must Thou char the wood ere Thou canst limn
    with it![4]

Fairy tales do not give us the answer. But maybe they can help us live with the question. And how else would you learn to live with Psyche's invisible Lover?

CHAPTER 11

NARROW IS THE WAY

If we commit to our spirituality — "keep our eyes on the vision and translate that vision into action" — will we find joy or suffering? Both, Brother David says, but it will be a different kind of joy and suffering. Comparing our commitment to the threshing of grain, he describes a narrowing that occurs. It is the nature of the spiritual path and cannot be bypassed, just as the "growing pain of going with the grain" cannot be avoided.

This narrowness, however, is not confining or limiting. Paradoxically, its focus opens us to an expansive vision. We set aside our need to make things go our way as more and more we trust that life itself is a gift and we find ourselves in the embrace of compassion. Instead of the never-ending anxiety of protecting what we have, we shift our attention to others. Wide new vistas of love and belonging open up to us. As this essay shows, there is a joy in the rhythm of this new commitment just as there is pain in clinging to old ways.

The people who wrote the Gospels and letters of the New Testament understood that the glory they recognized in Jesus was not the opposite of suffering: it was the fruit of his suffering. We should realize the truth of what they knew, because the way of the cross doesn't just belong to the life of Jesus. If we live the kind of life that

Jesus lived — the contemplative life of keeping the eyes continuously on the vision and of then translating that vision into everyday action — we will inevitably end up on the cross. We may be reluctant to accept this, but, in fact, there is no bypass. This is just a basic law of life.

In an essay entitled "The Joy in the Thought That It Is Not the Way Which Is Narrow, but the Narrowness Which Is the Way," the nineteenth-century Christian existentialist Søren Kierkegaard argues that the spiritual journey is not separate from the way it is traveled.[1] The way doesn't exist in the same sense that a road exists, regardless of whether anyone is traveling on it or not. It is the "how" of the traveling that makes it the path. When we speak of life as a way, the real question is, how am I to walk on that way; how am I to live my life?

Kierkegaard quotes Jesus: "For the gate is narrow and the way is hard, that leads to life" (Matt. 7:14). Again, "narrow" is not an adjective, describing the path; narrow is the path. The name of the path is narrow. Therefore, when life is narrow, we know it is the path. An alternative term frequently used in the Bible is "tribulation," which literally means "threshing the grain." The chaff flies away, and the grain falls through. We can't avoid tribulation; we can't avoid narrowness. Paradoxically, it is this realization that brings joy. We know what we must do: we must suffer.

Does our suffering increase as we move forward on the way? Is the way narrow only at the entrance? According to Kierkegaard, we suffer more and more. But what does this mean? A passage from the prologue of the Rule of St. Benedict, which may at first seem to contradict Kierkegaard, sees the suffering and the path from a different perspective. St. Benedict writes:

Therefore we intend to establish a school for the Lord's service. In drawing up its regulations, we hope to set down nothing harsh, nothing burdensome. The good of all concerned, however, may prompt a little strictness in order to amend faults and to safeguard love. Do not be daunted immediately by fear and run away from the road that leads to salvation. It is bound to be narrow at the outset. But as we progress in this way of life and in faith, we shall run on the path of God's commandments, our hearts overflowing with the inexpressible delight of love.

For me, any contradiction between St. Benedict and Kierkegaard is only superficial. Once we discover that narrowness is the way, we participate in the joy of understanding that it is so, which is also the "inexpressible delight" referred to by St. Benedict. It comes down to appreciating that life is a gift and that we have neither bought nor earned this gift of life.

Therefore we have a choice of two attitudes, both of which involve pain. We can suffer from anxiety because we don't trust that life is a good gift. Or, instead, we can exchange our anxiety for a different, more positive kind of suffering: that of compassion. This second, positive choice involves a growing pain, the joyful suffering of going with the grain, of realizing that it is narrowness that leads to life. In our preoccupation with having things go our way, we may balk at this opportunity to move freely with life's changes, especially those we consider harsh. Yet any pleasure we might hope to gain from anxiously protecting ourselves dims by comparison with a trusting attitude.

When His Holiness the Dalai Lama visited the United States in 1981, someone asked him, in a small audience, how it was that Buddhists have developed such a wonderful path for overcoming suffering, while Christians have been wallowing in their suffering for almost two thousand years. The Dalai Lama responded by saying, "It is not as easy as all that. Suffering is not overcome by leaving pain behind; suffering is overcome by bearing pain for others." And that is one of those answers that is as Christian as it is Buddhist. It is the basic statement that comes out of the fact that narrowness is the path.

CHAPTER 12

THE HOUSE OF HOPE

How much we are still in need of embracing the wisdom behind a question that Brother David raised in this essay almost thirty years ago: What kind of house can we build that could accommodate all those in our world who want to worship God? For Brother David, the answer was and still is a house of hope. Only hope can "build a roof without losing sight of the stars ... [and] walls without losing sight of our neighbors." Only hope can attempt to satisfy what he has called "the fullness of our longing and belonging."

When a word is being tossed around as much as "ecumenism" is being tossed around today, it is often helpful to look for its roots. The word "ecumenical" is rooted in the Greek word for "house." This is also true for the words "economy" and "ecology." All three terms point to a reality that Gary Snyder calls "Earth Household." As we become aware that our earth is one great household, we must face the challenge to live accordingly. This demands a new relationship to our environment based on reverence and frugality; it demands what Fritz Schumacher calls "economics as if people mattered" (*Small Is Beautiful*), and it will make us raise the basic question of ecumenism: What kind of worldwide house could possibly accommodate all those who, in so many different ways, want to worship God?

The answer I would like to suggest is this: Our house of worldwide worship will have to be a house of hope. Only hope can build that house, because only hope, rightly understood, can hold together the paradox of religion. Being religious means both that we find a home for the heart and that, in T. S. Eliot's words, "We shall not cease from exploration."[1] St. Stephen, the first Christian martyr, died for the truth that God does not dwell in houses built by human hands (Acts 7:48ff.). Before his death he quoted from the Old Testament — " 'What kind of house will you build for me?' says the Lord" (1 Kings 17:24) — as witness that being religious means being on the move.

163

> We must be still and still moving
> Into another intensity
> For a further union, a deeper communion
> Through the dark cold and the empty desolation.[2]

And yet when in the midst of that empty desolation we catch a glimpse of the divine Light, our heart cries out, like Peter on Mount Tabor, "How good it is for us to be here!" (Matt. 7:4). And the very next thought is, "Let us build here!" In the Old Testament, too, Jacob calls out: "How awe-inspiring is this place! This is none other than the house of God, and this is the gate of heaven" (Gen. 29:17). He, too, immediately thinks of building. He sets up the stone that was his pillow while he had the dream vision, and says, "This stone, which I have set up as a monument, shall be God's house" (Gen. 28:22).

If we look closely, these two Bible stories express an insight that belongs to all religious traditions: only hope can build God's house. Jacob sets up a milestone on the road, as it were, and calls it "Bethel," the House of God. And the three tabernacles that Peter offers to build on Mount Tabor are *sukkoth,* wayfarers' tents, which faithful Jews still build year after year to remember the time of their wilderness wandering, when in the midst of the "dark cold and the empty desolation," God's Presence was closer than ever. The house that hope builds combines in a unique way the security of love and the adventure of faith.

This theme is expressed with great tenderness in the traditional rule for building the *sukkoth,* that little booth adorned with fruit and branches where a Jewish family will eat and drink and sing together for nine days each year to celebrate the Feast of Tabernacles. Even the poorest will build that little festive tent. They will build it on the landing of some fire escape, if they have no other space, in the crowded tenement houses of the Lower East Side of Manhattan. And this is the rule for building it: Make the walls not too dense; you should still be able to look through to see your neighbor. And make the roof loose enough to look through to the stars.

Two opposing tendencies within us make us want to break these simple rules: our tendency to drift — for the drifter doesn't build at all — and our tendency to entrench ourselves firmly behind solid walls. Both are forms of fear in disguise. We fear to be still, and we fear to be "still and still moving." Hope alone "moves perpetually in its stillness."[3] Hope is the daughter of a twofold courage, the courage to build and the courage to build lightly. Hope will build a roof without losing sight of the stars; hope will build walls without losing sight of our neighbors. That is why hope alone is able to build the house of ecumenism, where God truly dwells with us, because we truly dwell together.

Drifters cannot build. They lack the anchorage one needs to be creative. True hope is so firmly anchored in the courage and trust of faith that it will set afloat a whole fleet of new hopes each time old hopes go down. But drifters don't have the courage to give shape to their dreams, to build as they travel. They may spend the night under a roof that is not their own, but when the morning comes they will drift on, fearful to commit themselves.

And there are others who will indeed build. Fearful of being on the way, they entrench themselves. They clearly shape their hopes but, clinging desperately to these very hopes, in the end they lose all hope. True Hope shines bright as a star above a shipwreck after all our other hopes have sunk. If we confuse our transient hopes with the real Hope, we build so tight a roof that we can no longer see the stars. God's mercy will have to break up that roof above us.

When I meet drifters, I admire in them the courage it takes to keep moving. When I see builders, even the builders of far too solid walls, I admire their courage to build. Isn't it asking too much that one should have the courage for both? Yet nothing short of it will do for men and women of hope. That is what we must do if the whole earth is to become "a house of prayer for all the peoples" (Isa. 56:7). "Unless the Lord build the house, they labor in vain that build it" (Ps. 127:1), and the plans of the Divine Architect are as far beyond all our planning as True Hope is beyond our ordinary hopes.

CHAPTER 13

THE PRICE OF PEACE

Nothing in this essay about our role in creating peace in the world is beyond our reach. Brother David simply asks us to start with our own attitudes and our own life choices: one step at a time, one person at a time. These are the seeds for change that he sowed when he offered these thoughts in 1985. He does not believe that it is easy to get these seeds to take root, but he does trust Religion's unique ability to give us support in our endeavors. At the mystical core of religious traditions, he reminds us, is the universal experience of belonging and of peace. We need to take courage — and direction — from this experience.

I would like to share with you something that is very simple but also very difficult: simple things often are. It is an invitation to pay the price for peace. We all know that peace is an exceedingly high good. But for an exceedingly high good we should expect to pay an exceedingly high price. I would like to explore with you what the price of peace is, and then to suggest why, in my opinion, the only force in human life that can generate enough energy to pay that price is religion. Obviously, to do this we will have to redefine religion a bit and look at what it is that makes religion religious, because it is by no means automatically religious. In fact, I tend to think it is automatically irreligious unless we do something to make it religious.

I have four fairly simple points that you can augment or change, but that will give us a ground plan for exploring the price we have to pay for peace.

First, we have to face our failure to create a peaceful world. We have all had a part in creating this world. It costs us a great deal to admit that each one of us is implicated. But as long as we cannot admit this, we remain very far from peace. We remain in a world we have divided into "us" and "them": "us" the good ones and "them" the ones who present the problem and obstacle to peace, the enemy. It makes no difference who "they" are — they can be political heads of states, terrorists, liberals, conservatives, rich or poor, young or old. If we face the fact that we are one, that "they" are "us," that the face of the enemy is our own face, then we will have reached the first basis for peace.

I assure you this is difficult. I find myself continuously sliding into, maybe not talking, but at least thinking about "they" — if only "they" didn't give us all that trouble we would have peace on earth. To bring home this fact that we are one, at the beginning of Lent one year I found a photograph of some people who for me are "they." That picture became my Lenten pin-up. I looked at it every day, and gradually "they" became "us." I suggest you think of some creative way to help you accept the fact that we are one: pick your "theys" and identify with them in some way or other.

Second, after we can acknowledge that it is we who have failed to make peace and we who can make peace, then we obviously have to rise to our responsibility and do something. People typically respond, "What on earth can I do?" That's a great starting place. You have marked out your homework. You know the question; now find out the answer. Get together with someone else and ask the same question — two heads are better than one, as they say. If the two of you cannot come up with something, ask two others. Now, there will be four people. Imagine the whole world getting together and asking what we can do — the solution would not be very far away.

The moment you ask the question, you will find things you can do. Very simple things. Here is one example. Many years ago I was at the ordination of a Buddhist abbot. It was a very solemn occasion — incense, flowers, gold brocade, candles — and in the midst of the ceremony somebody's beeper on their electronic wristwatch went off. You aren't even supposed to wear a wristwatch in a zendo, so it was very embarrassing. Everybody was looking around: "Who is the poor guy to whom this has happened?" It turned out to be the abbot who was being ordained. He interrupted the whole ceremony and said, "This was no accident. I have set this alarm because I have made a vow that every day at twelve noon, regardless of what I am doing, I will stop and think thoughts of peace." And he invited everybody there to think thoughts of peace with him for one minute.

We can all do something like that: set our little alarm clocks, and if that interrupts a meeting say we're terribly sorry, but we've made a vow to think thoughts of peace at that time. We could even get bells rung. A village on the south island of New Zealand has done that every day at twelve noon. Maybe you can find some little village or neighborhood where you can ring the bells or a radio station that is willing to play beautiful bells for half a minute at twelve noon. Provide them with a half-minute tape of bells — something that will remind people over and over again. That's one creative idea. You may have thousands of others.

Now, having faced the fact that we are one and having risen to our responsibility, we need to see that we are the problem — not only in general but also specifically. Most of us in the first world are exploiting the third world. So the third, very difficult step is to give up some privilege we enjoy at the expense of others. For most of us, the willingness may be all we can muster to begin with. But we can be willing to make as a motto for ourselves what the first canonized saint of the United States, Mother Seton, said two hundred years ago: "Live simply so that others may simply live."

The fourth step is to run the risk involved in everything above. In the kind of world in which we live it is very risky to lead a moral life, because morality — and some people don't like to hear this — is always unilateral. You do not make it a condition for your not stealing that others will not steal from you. You do not make it a condition that you will live a moral life provided others behave morally to you. We know it from our personal lives, but in public we always want bilaterality. We do not want to be unilaterally honest or peaceful. That's a great risk. If we dare to do it, it will cost us no less than everything. But it will be worth it. It will be a breaking of our heart. As Marilyn Ferguson said so beautifully, depression is sorrow that doesn't go all the way to breaking our heart. But if we allow our hearts to be broken they will be broken open, not broken down, open to embrace everyone.

I have a small personal experience that fits in here. For a fairly long time I had continuous nosebleeds, which began to build up until, at midnight Mass one Christmas, the whole thing came to a climax. We wear white at midnight Mass, so a nosebleed can be a big problem. It started just before we went in, and by the end of the ceremony I was a bloody mess. Afterward I went to a friend in whom I have great confidence, and he said, "I'll pray with you about it, but first let's examine what's happening. I get the impression that you are quite exposed to a lot of things going on in the world. In other words, you are sticking your nose into a lot of things — and it breaks your heart. But you don't allow your heart to bleed, and so your nose starts bleeding instead. Why don't you unite your heart with the heart of Jesus and let it bleed, and then maybe your nose will stop bleeding."

Well, whenever I manage to do this my nose does stop bleeding. We live in a kind of world in which we need to let our hearts bleed. That will free us from a depression and nosebleeds and all sorts of other things. It will be a sharing of blood, a kind of blood donor program. We need something of that sort.

Even if the breaking of our heart leads to our physical end, to final suffering, it will be a triumph. You may have heard of this story — I won't name the country because it is really a universal story — where the police herded thousands of people from a peace rally into a stadium, as a temporary prison, and the people all sang. They sang and sang and the police didn't know what to do with prisoners who sang. The leader who was playing the guitar and singing got his hands smashed, but he kept singing. Then they tried to smash his teeth so he couldn't sing any more, and then his head. Before long this brutality — which he did not resist — killed him, but the stadium continued singing. Now this is the story of Christ's death and resurrection in a contemporary version. And it's the story of Orpheus, who was torn into pieces by furious enemies, but who was thereby distributed so that now he sings, as Rilke says, even in trees and in rocks and in lions. Everything sings. If we allow ourselves to be broken and distributed like bread then everything will become peaceful. It can go that far.

But why do I say that only Religion can give us the energy to pay this price? It is because I do not identify Religion with religions. If I did, I couldn't possibly say this. But there must be some relationship between what I call Religion and the religions. That relationship is what makes religions religious.

When you look at the heart of every religious tradition, you see that the starting point in each is the profound limitless sense of belonging. There is no religion in the world that would not subscribe to this. God does not need to be introduced here, but if you want to make this introduction, God is the reference point for that sense of belonging. This belonging comes first. It is not something you find out there; it's something you experience inside, personally. And in these moments in which you personally experience that deep sense of belonging, you are at peace. Religion is peace, because that experience of limitless belonging is one of tranquility and security, and it is experienced in an attitude of nonviolence. Violence makes no sense at all in that context.

We are obviously a long way from *this religious experience* at the heart of every religious tradition to the *institutions of religion* that we find today. But we can at least acknowledge the direction we know we should be headed toward and reflect this direction in each of the components of every religion. Our *doctrines* can reflect an interpretation of that sense of belonging or peace in all its different aspects. Our *rituals* can celebrate that sense of universal belonging, of peace, tranquility, security, and nonviolence. And our *morality* can support our willingness to live out that peace, to make it a reality. This is morality — the commitment to living out of a sense of belonging, to realizing that peace.

The means by which we can measure how close religions come to being religious is by how truly they realize peace. Some of them limit that commitment. "Yes, we live out our belonging, but these people are the ones who belong to us and under these conditions — and then there are all those people outside." When these limits are no longer drawn, when the commitment to living that sense of belonging becomes universal, then we may be able to say our particular religious tradition is religious. In the course of history, religions have become more religious and then less religious, and then they reform and again become more religious. It goes up and down. We should expect that. If it happens in our own personal lives why should it not happen in our religious traditions?

Now, if we are part of a particular religious tradition, we have both the responsibility and the right to use its structures to bring about the best goals for which those structures have been set up. We can use them to bring about peace, and sometimes the structures do more than one individual can. But before we can mobilize these structures we have to make our religions religious. That is the great task for anyone who stands in any particular religious tradition.

If we understand religion in this way, we can see why it can and will give us the power to pay the price of peace. If we really experience that oneness with all, that belonging to all which is the basic religious insight, then we will be able to face the fact that whatever shortcomings there are belong to all. The oneness that stands at the core of the religious experience simply eliminates "we" and "they." And if we accept the inner authority that comes from our religious experience, then we will have the courage to rise to our responsibility. Authority that comes from either above or below is still an authority that comes from without. The real paradigm shift is when authority comes from within. This is where the great paradigm shift is taking place at the present moment within the religions themselves, all over the world. Each of us bestows authority on all the authorities we recognize, and unless we bestow authority on them we will not recognize them as authorities. But we can also recognize, as religious language puts it, God the Divine within us. This is actually the only place where we can recognize the Divine: We never find it outside unless we first find it within us. We are divine; we share the Divine. It is on that authority alone that we can accept other authority.

If we are one with all, then we will hurt when others hurt — and then we will be willing to give up privileges. We will be willing to pay the price. We will be able to sing to the end, and we will have the trust and courage and knowledge — deep, ingrained knowledge — that this singing will go on regardless of whether somebody smashes our hands that play the instrument.

So finally, I would ask you to address yourselves to four questions and to commit yourselves to what we have been talking about:

- Do you commit yourself to live from that heart of hearts where we are one with all?

- Do you commit yourself to rise to your responsibility, to go one little step at a time on the road of peace?

- Do you commit yourself to giving up as best you can complicity in exploitation?

- Do you, remembering, as T. S. Eliot put it, "a condition of complete simplicity, costing not less than everything," commit yourself to the risk of making peace happen?

If you will do all this, we are very well on the road of peace.

CHAPTER 14

GIVING THANKS FOR ALL THE LITTLE (AND BIG) THINGS IN LIFE

If Brother David's spirituality had to be condensed into one word, one practice, one concept, it would be gratefulness. For him, gratefulness is our heartiest response to the gift of life: "Our full appreciation of our very aliveness, of that which is altogether unearned, utterly gratuitous: life, existence, ultimate belonging." All-encompassing, this gratefulness implies for him a trust in the giver that is the core of faith; an openness for surprise that is the essence of hope; and a "yes" to our belonging that is love.

While our peak moments may be our most vivid experiences of gratefulness, Brother David knows well that we can and need to nurture our sense of gratefulness. In the busyness of our lives, gratefulness is not necessarily a spontaneous reaction. We have to familiarize our heart, our mind, and our will with it. We need to practice gratefulness to make it part of who we are.

Brother David has written an entire book on this topic. In this essay, he gives a practice for beginners. He starts with surprise and the art of not taking life for granted.

For a fuller understanding of gratefulness, see *Gratefulness, the Heart of Prayer* or go to *www.gratefulness.org*.

Have you ever noticed how your eyes open a bit wider when you are surprised? It is as if you had been asleep, merely daydreaming or sleepwalking through some routine activity, and then you hear your favorite tune on the radio, or you look up from the puddles on the parking lot and see a rainbow, or the telephone rings and it's the voice of an old friend, and all of a sudden you're awake. Even an unwelcome surprise shakes us out of complacency and makes us come alive. We may not like it at first, but looking back, we can always recognize it as a gift. Humdrum equals deadness; surprise equals life. In fact, my favorite name for the One I worship in wonder — the only name that does not limit God — is Surprise.

Right this moment, as I remember spiritual giants I have been privileged to meet — Mother Teresa, Thomas Merton, Dorothy Day, His Holiness the Dalai Lama — I can still feel the life energy they radiated. But how did they come by this vitality? There is no lack of surprises in this world, but such radiant aliveness is rare. What I observed was that these people were all profoundly grateful, and then I understood the secret.

A surprise does not make us automatically alive. Aliveness is a matter of give-and-take, of response. If we allow surprise merely to baffle us, it will stun us and stunt our growth. Instead, every surprise is a challenge to trust in life and so to grow. Surprise is a seed. Gratefulness sprouts when we rise to the challenge of surprise. The great ones in the realm of Spirit are so intensely alive because they are so deeply grateful.

Gratefulness can be improved by practice. But where shall beginners begin? The obvious starting point is surprise. You will find that you can grow the seeds of gratefulness just by making room. If surprise happens when something unexpected shows up, let's not expect anything at all. Let's follow Alice Walker's advice: "Expect nothing. Live frugally on surprise."

To expect nothing may mean not taking for granted that your car will start when you turn the key. Try this and you will be surprised by a marvel of technology worthy of sincere gratitude. Or you may not be thrilled by your job, but if for a moment you can stop taking it for granted, you will taste the surprise of having a job at all, while millions are unemployed. If this makes you feel a flicker of gratefulness, you'll be a little more joyful all day, a little more alive.

Once we stop taking things for granted, our own body can become one of the most surprising things of all. It never ceases to amaze me that my body both produces and destroys 15 million red blood cells every second. Fifteen million! That's nearly twice the census figure for New York City. I am told that the blood vessels in my body, if lined up end to end, would reach around the world. Yet my heart needs only one minute to pump my blood through this filigree network and back again. It has been doing so minute by minute, day by day, for more than eighty years and still keeps pumping away at a hundred thousand heartbeats every twenty-four hours. Obviously this is a matter of life and death for me, yet I have no idea how it works and it seems to work amazingly well in spite of my ignorance.

I do not know how my eyes adapt, yet when I chant by candlelight they are a hundred thousand times more sensitive to light than when I read outdoors on the porch at noon. I wouldn't know how to give instructions to the 35 million digestive glands in my stomach for digesting one single strawberry; fortunately, they know how to do their job without my advice. When I think of this as I sit down to eat, my heart brims with gratefulness.

In those moments, I can identify with the Psalmist who cried out in amazement, "I am fearfully and wonderfully made" (Ps. 139:14). From there it is only a small step to seeing the whole universe and every smallest part of it as surprising. From the humble starting point of daily surprises, the practice of gratefulness leads to these transcendent heights. Thomas Carlyle pointed to these peaks of spiritual awareness when he wrote, "Worship is transcendent wonder" — transcendent surprise.

A Few Tips for Offline Practice

+ Surprise is the seed of gratefulness. Become aware of surprises. Relish surprises as life's gifts.

+ Learn to find the gift within every gift: opportunity — mostly the opportunity to enjoy, always the opportunity to learn.

+ Practice availing yourself of opportunities. Do everything gratefully. Do something simply to celebrate gratefulness.

+ Share your experience with others. Share joys and double them. Share pain and cut it in half.

+ Enjoy the energy boost grateful living gives you. Dare to tackle new projects. Taste the joy of turning feeling good into doing good.

CHAPTER 15

A NEW REASON
FOR GRATITUDE

Normally, we associate gratefulness with a positive event, and, in fact, Brother David frequently urges his audiences to begin the practice of gratefulness when life is going well. But what happens when the worst occurs? Is there any room for grate-fulness at a time when we are suffering a terrible loss, illness, or disruption in our lives? What about on such a day as September 11, 2001?

This essay shows how completely gratitude is at the center of Brother David's spiritual way. He speaks of the "gift within the gift," but what could possibly be the gift of the violence of 9/11? For Brother David, it was the opportunity for us all to finally recognize the futility of violence. He hoped our response would be to make it the last act of violence. That has not happened, but the calm, the courage, the trust and love that is so much a part of gratefulness can still offset the fear, panic, suspicion, and confusion that exists because of violence.

Brother David considers the spiritual task of our time to be rerooting what has been cut off from its roots. This re-rooting includes ourselves, so that we become spiritually whole, alive in mind, body, and spirit. Gratefulness is the "how" of this spiritual work — a powerful antidote to violence — as he demonstrates in this essay.

This morning I buried a chipmunk. The cat's teeth had left no marks. The cheeky fellow seemed to just have curled up to sleep in the hole I had dug between early chrysanthemums. As I piled a few trowels full of soil on this little grave, I remembered with a smile childhood games of burying dead birds and bugs and mice. Suddenly I thought of humans — thousands upon thousands — whom no one ever buried, because not even their bodies were left, victims of violence from Hiroshima and Nagasaki to lower Manhattan. Gratitude? The very word seems utterly out of place, even offensive, under the given circumstances.

And yet that we speak of "given" circumstances is significant. Whatever is given is gift; and the appropriate response to any gift is gratitude. But what could be the gift in this case? The gift we were given by the Wake-up Call of September 11 is an unprecedented opportunity. The gift within every gift is opportunity. For us, these days, it is the opportunity to wake up — wake up to the madness of violence and counterviolence. After all, we witnessed merely the most recent link in a chain of revenge for revenge. This recent retaliation is certainly not the first, but it gives us a unique opportunity to wake up and to make it the last.

Strange though it is, many of us were able to ignore the vicious circle of violence against violence — our own and that of others — as long as it was happening far away. We were asleep. This was a rough awakening. What now? We can show ourselves grateful for the Wake-up Call by staying awake, by acting wakefully. A danger recognized and faced is cut in half. The danger is violence — regardless of who commits it, terrorists or legitimate governments. No rhetoric, no posturing can any longer obscure the fact that violence breeds violence. We must break that cycle of madness.

Violence has its roots in every heart. It is in my own heart that I must recognize fear, agitation, coldness, alienation, and the impulse to blind anger. Here in my heart I can turn fear into courageous trust, agitation and confusion into stillness, isolation into a sense of belonging, alienation into love, and irrational reaction into Common Sense. The creative imagination of gratefulness will suggest to each one of us how to go about this task. I will list here five small gestures that have helped me personally show my gratitude for the Wake-up Call and stay awake.

All gratitude expresses trust. Suspicion will not even recognize a gift as gift: who can prove that it isn't a lure, a bribe, a trap? Gratefulness has the courage to trust and so overcomes fear. The air has been electrified by fearfulness these days, a fearfulness fostered and manipulated by politicians and the media. There lies our greatest danger: fear perpetuates violence. Mobilize the courage of your heart, as the truly awake ones are doing. *Say one word today that gives a fearful person courage.*

Because gratitude expresses courage, it spreads calm. Calm of this kind is quite compatible with deep emotions. In fact, the mass hysteria rampant all around betrays confusion rather than deep feeling — superficial agitation rather than a deep current of compassion. Join the truly compassionate ones who are calm and strong. From the stillness of your heart's core reach out. *Calmly hold someone's hand today and spread calm.*

When you are grateful, your heart is open — open toward others, open for surprise. In the days since the Wake-up Call we have seen remarkable examples of this openness: strangers helping strangers often in heroic ways. Others turn away, isolate themselves, dare even less than at other times to look at each other. Violence begins with isolation. Break this pattern. Make contact with people whom you normally ignore — eye-contact at least — with the agent at the toll booth or the parking lot attendant, the elderly person slowly making her way up the steps. *Look this person in the eyes today and realize that there are no strangers.*

You can feel either grateful or alienated, but never both at the same time. Gratefulness drives out alienation; there is not room for both in the same heart. When you are grateful you know that you belong to a network of give-and-take and you say "yes" to that belonging. This "yes" is the essence of love. You need no words to express it; a smile will do to put your "yes" into action. Don't let it matter to you whether or not the other one smiles back. *Give someone an unexpected smile today and so contribute your share to peace on earth.*

What your gratefulness does for yourself is as important as what it does for others. Gratefulness boosts your sense of belonging; your sense of belonging in turn boosts your Common Sense. Your "yes" to belonging attunes you to the common concerns shared by all human beings. After the Wake-up Call, nothing else makes sense but Common Sense. We have only one enemy, our common enemy: violence. Common Sense tells us: we can stop violence only by stopping to act violently; war is no way to peace. *Listen to the news today and put at least one item to the test of Common Sense.*

The five steps I am suggesting here are small, but they work. It helps that they are small: anyone can take them. Imagine a country whose citizens — maybe even its leaders — are brave, calm, and open toward each other; a country whose people realize that all human beings belong together as one family and must act accordingly; a country guided by Common Sense. To the extent to which we show ourselves not hateful but grateful this becomes reality. Who would have foreseen that gratitude could shine forth with such new brightness in these dark days? May it light our way.

183

— September 2001

NOTES

Chapter 1: Spirituality as Common Sense

Reprinted, with revisions, from *The Quest* 3, no. 2 (Summer 1990): 12–17.

1. Excerpts from "Vacillations" by William Butler Yeats, reprinted with the permission of Scribner, an imprint of Simon & Schuster Adult Publishing Group, from *The Collected Works of W. B. Yeats,* vol. 1: *The Poems, Revised,* edited by Richard J. Finneran. Copyright © 1933 by The Macmillan Company; copyright renewed © 1961 by Bertha Georgie Yeats. All rights reserved.

2. "The Joy of Fishes," in *The Way of Chuang Tzu,* trans. Thomas Merton (New York: New Directions Publishing, 1965), 97–99. copyright © 1965 by The Abbey of Gethsemani. Reprinted by permission of New Directions Publishing Corp.

Chapter 2: The Monk in Us

Reprinted from *Epiphany,* Spring 1981.

Chapter 3: Art and the Sacred

Reprinted from *Lindisfarne Letter,* no. 6, 1978.

1. Excerpts from "East Coker" in *Four Quartets,* copyright 1940 by T. S. Eliot and renewed 1968 by Esme Valerie Eliot, reprinted by permission of Harcourt, Inc. Excerpts from "The Dry Salvages" in Four Quartets, copyright 1941 by T. S. Eliot and renewed 1969 by Esme Valerie Eliot, reprinted by permission of Harcourt, Inc. Excerpts from "Little Gidding" in *Four Quartets,* copyright 1942 by T. S. Eliot and renewed 1970 by Esme Valerie Eliot, reprinted by permission of Harcourt, Inc.

2. Excerpts from "Precious Five" by W. H. Auden, from *W. H. Auden: Collected Poems,* ed. Edward Mendelson (New York: Random House, 1945).

3. From *Four Quartets.*
4. Ibid.
5. From *The Ninth Elegy* by Rainer Maria Rilke, *Duino Elegies,* trans. Brother David or as in *Gratefulness,* trans. J. B. Lcishman and Stephen Spender (New York: W. W. Norton, 1939), copyright 1967 by Stephen Spender and J. B. Leishman.

Chapter 4: Sacramental Life

Reprinted from *Warm Wind: The Chinook Learning Community Journal* 2, no. 1 (1979).

1. Eugene O'Neil, "A Long Day's Journey into Night," Act 4.
2. From C. S. Lewis, *Perelandra* (New York: Macmillan 1947), 230.
3. O'Neil, "A Long Day's Journey into Night."

Chapter 5: Views of the Cosmos

Reprinted from *Parabola* 2, no. 3 (1977): 6–13.

1. Maria Leach, *Beginning: Creation Myths Around the World* (New York: Funk & Wagnalls, 1956.)
2. Paul Radin, *Primitive Man as Philosopher* (New York: Appleton & Co., 1927).
3. Leach, *Beginning.*
4. John L. McKenzie, *The Two-Edged Sword: An Interpretation of the Old Testament* (Milwaukee: Bruce Publishing Co., 1956.)
5. Henri Frankfort and H. A. Groenewegen-Frankfort, *The Intellectual Adventure of Ancient Man: An Essay on Speculative Thought in the Ancient Near East* (Chicago: University of Chicago Press, 1957).
6. Erwin Schroedinger, *Nature and the Greeks* (London and New York: Cambridge University Press, 1954).
7. Frankfort and Groenewegen-Frankfort, *The Intellectual Adventure of Ancient Man.*
8. From Gerard Manley Hopkins's poem "That Nature Is a Heraclitean Fire and of the Comfort of the Resurrection," reprinted from *Parabola* 2, no. 3 (1977): 6–13.

Chapter 6: The Mystical Core of Organized Religion

Reprinted from *New Realities* 10, no. 4 (March–April 1990): 35–37.

1. From an unpublished translation, with the kind permission of Coleman Barks and John Moyne, whose volume of Rumi translations is entitled *This Longing* (Putney, Vt.: Threshold, 1988).

2. Ibid.

Chapter 7: The God Problem

Reprinted from *Spirituality and Health* (June 2004); "This Is It" is an excerpt from "The Great Circle Dance," an essay that further develops Brother David's view on world religions. It can be read at *www.gratefulness.org*.

Chapter 8: Shadows

Reprinted from *The Sun*, 137 (April 1987): 20–23) and originally given as a talk at a 1986 Sufi retreat in Lebanon Springs, New York.

Chapter 9: Learning to Die

Reprinted from *Parabola* 2, no. 1 (Winter 1977): 22–31. Note from the *Parabola* editors: "In response to our invitation Brother David told us that he did indeed have something that he would like to say about death, but that he would prefer to tell it rather than write it. This essay was an edited version of what he had to say, and it retains an oral quality. It thus should be read as much with the ears as with the eyes."

Chapter 10: Paths of Obedience

Reprinted from *Parabola* 5 (August 1980): 33–43.

1. Francis Thompson, "The Hound of Heaven" in *The Oxford Book of English Mystical Verse,* ed. Nicholson E. Lee (New York: Oxford University Press, 1969), 409–15.

2. T. S. Eliot, "Little Gidding" in *Four Quartets,* New York: Harcourt, Inc., 1941, by T. S. Eliot and renewed 1969 by Esme Valerie Eliot, reprinted by permission of Harcourt, Inc.

3. Thompson, "The Hound of Heaven."

4. Ibid.

Chapter II: Narrow Is the Way

Reprinted with permission from *Speaking of Silence: Christians and Buddhists in Dialogue,* © 2005 by Vajradhatu Publications, 2nd edition. *Speaking of Silence* is available directly from the publisher at *www.shambhalashop.com* and through *Gratefulness.org*'s Amazon portal.

  1. Kierkegaard's article appeared in *Edifying Discourses: A Selection,* trans. David F. Swenson and Lillian Marvin Swenson (New York: Harper & Brothers, 1958).

Chapter I2: The House of Hope

Reprinted from *Integral Yoga* 10, no. 4 (August 1979): 10–11 and 25.

  1. Excerpts from "Little Gidding" in *Four Quartets,* copyright 1942 by T. S. Eliot and renewed 1970 by Esme Valerie Eliot, reprinted by permission of Harcourt, Inc.
  2. Excerpts from "East Coker" in *Four Quartets,* copyright 1940 by T. S. Eliot and renewed 1968 by Esme Valerie Eliot, reprinted by permission of Harcourt, Inc.
  3. Excerpts from "Burnt Norton" in Four Quartets, copyright 1940 by T. S. Eliot and renewed 1968 by Esme Valerie Eliot, reprinted by permission of Harcourt, Inc.

Chapter I3: The Price of Peace

This article was excerpted from Brother David's talk at the "Spirit of Peace" conference held in Amsterdam in March 1985. It was originally published in the Findhorn Foundation's *One Earth* 5, no. 5 (July–August 1985): 11–13, with the permission of the Agape Forum for Art, which organized the conference for the benefit of the United Nations University for Peace.

Chapter I4: Giving Thanks for All the Little (and Big) Things in Life

Reprinted from *Spirituality and Health* (Winter 2002): 34–37.

Chapter I5: A New Reason for Gratitude

Reprinted from *www.gratefulness.org.*

Of Related Interest

Henri J. M. Nouwen
LIFE OF THE BELOVED
Spiritual Living in a Secular World

Over 200,000 copies in print!

"One day while walking on Columbus Avenue in New York City, Fred turned to me and said, 'Why don't you write something about the spiritual life for me and my friends?'

"Fred's question became more than the intriguing suggestion of a young New York intellectual. It became the plea that arose on all sides — wherever I was open to hear it. And, in the end, it became for me the most pertinent and the most urgent of all demands: 'Speak to us about God.'"

— From the prologue

"Gentle and searching. This Crossroad book is a spiritual primer for anyone seeking God."
— The Other Side

0-8245-1986-8, paperback

Of Related Interest

Joan Chittister
THE RULE OF BENEDICT
Insights for the Ages

The Benedictine way, the author contends, "is the spirituality of the twenty-first century because it deals with issues facing us now — stewardship, relationships, authority, community, balance, work, simplicity, prayer, and spiritual and psychological development."

0-8245-2503-5, paperback

Check your local bookstore for availability.
To order directly from the publisher,
please call 1-800-707-0670 for Customer Service
or visit our Web site at *www.cpcbooks.com.*
For catalog orders, please send your request to the address below.

THE CROSSROAD PUBLISHING COMPANY
16 Penn Plaza, Suite 1550
New York, NY 10001

crossroad